Sexual Essays

Gender, Desire, and Nakedness

James Giles

Hamilton Books

Lanham • Boulder • New York • Toronto • Plymouth, UK

4501 Forbes Boulevard, Suite 200, Lanham, Maryland 20706
Hamilton Books Acquisitions Department (301) 459-3366

Unit A, Whitacre Mews, 26-34 Stannary Street,
London SE11 4AB, United Kingdom

Printed in the United States of America
British Library Cataloguing in Publication Information Available

Library of Congress Control Number: 2016963125
ISBN: 978-0-7618-6889-7 (pbk : alk. paper)—ISBN: 978-0-7618-6890-3 (electronic)

Cover image: A detail of *Mars and Venus, Allegory of Peace*, (1770) by Louis Jean François Lagrenée. Digital image courtesy of the Getty's Open Content Program.

∞™ The paper used in this publication meets the minimum requirements of American National Standard for Information Sciences Permanence of Paper for Printed Library Materials, ANSI/NISO Z39.48-1992.

Contents

Preface

Sexuality is a basic feature of human life. Gender, sexual and romantic attraction, sexual excitement, and sexual desire and fantasies all move in various degrees through our daily awareness. However, despite this pervasiveness, there is much disagreement surrounding the nature of things sexual. This disagreement is one of the things that makes the study of sexuality fascinating. For if sexuality is such a basic feature of our lives, then it is puzzling that people have such divergent views about what it involves. Something being fundamental to human life or being regularly in our awareness seems to imply that everybody should know about it. But then how can people disagree so strongly? Further, not only are the views divergent, but they are often emotionally charged and tenaciously held.

It is difficult to say why exactly this disparity of views and high emotional investment should be the case. But one likely reason is that sexuality is a deeply personal topic. Early in life people become aware that there is something crucial about being one sex rather than another, that something about the genitals—those parts of the body that make us the sex we are—means they not to be exposed or publicly touched, and that sexual interaction is strangely taboo and something to be hidden and not discussed openly. Further, the prescriptions and innuendos that convey such messages are typically permeated with moralistic and religious overtones. Even sex education, which typically is both too little and too late, does not seem to change this basic picture.

Much of this, it would seem, provides fertile ground for people coming up furtively with their own ideas, while at the same time making it difficult for them to see through the infused moralistic and religious elements that might determine their views. And scholars, of course, are not immune to this. Such a state of affairs can easily lead to all sorts of views about sexuality while at the same time tying them to anxieties, guilt, and other emotional elements.

This does not mean that all points of discrepancy can be traced back to such concerns. For there are, of course, legitimate intellectual disagreements. There are, for example, different theoretical approaches, different ways of interpreting the data, and so on. But even here it is not difficult to discern the uneasiness or moralistic apprehensions that at least partially drive the view being put forward.

The reason I am drawing attention to all of this is simply by way of preparation for the polemic nature of the essays that follow. This book contains a series of interrelated essays, each of which deals with a central topic in human sexuality. Within each essay I present and argue for my own view on a particular issue, but do so in the wake of critiques aimed at other views. For the person coming to these sorts of discussions for the first time, it might well be perplexing to find that there could be such a basic disparity of views. I hope, however, that the points just made might throw some light on this.

I start off this series of discussions in the first essay by looking at the nature of gender. One of the reasons for the disagreements here, I feel, has to do with the fact that in English we have two words, namely "sex" or "gender," that have senses that are used interchangeably but which some people feel refer to different phenomena, or at least which they want to refer to different phenomena. People arguing for this try to redefine "gender" exclusively in terms of something like cultural expectations for masculinity and femininity. I reject this view, along with the more radical position that cultural expectations for men and women are not separable from physiology, showing the confusions that such positions involve. I criticize the attempt to define gender in terms of gender identity, along with the attempt to define gender identity in terms of gender role behaviour, showing how both these attempts are based on inconsistencies. I then look at what the phenomenon of transsexualism can bring to the discussion of gender.

From the meaning of "gender" I turn to the erotic meaning of the sexual positions. For it is just in these interactions that the meaning of gender comes to expression. But what is the purpose of there being different sexual positions? The human use of a variety of positions stands in stark contrast to most other species that typically employ only one position. Some scholars have argued that their purpose is to display various interpersonal attitudes, for example, dominance and submission, while others have suggested they are a means for achieving effective sexual stimulation.

Although these elements are frequently attributed to a sexual position, they are not erotic meanings in themselves. For positions engaged in for these reasons are not engaged in for erotic reasons. Through an analysis of the *Kāma Sūtra* I argue that the meaning of "desirously entering into each other" is what remains once the interpersonal orientation and other meanings have been removed.

But if the meaning of desirously entering into each other is the erotic meaning behind the sexual positions, where does this desire come from? This is the question I turn to in Essay 3. Some scholars attempt to explain sexual desire by claiming that it is biologically driven. A common position here is that sex hormones play a necessary causal role. Yet, as I try to show, the evidence for this is inadequate. With males the loss of sexual desire following hormonal changes can easily be explained in terms of social stigmas that are attached to the physiological situation. Concerning females, the relevance of sex hormones here is even more unclear. Research with non-human primates, I argue, supports this view of the non-essential relation of sex hormones to sexual desire.

I then present a phenomenology or experiential account of sex hormones, showing a possible non-essential relation between sex hormones and sexual desire. This suggests that sexual desire has its origin in the meanings we give our biology and not in our biology itself.

Scholars who reject the biological view of sexual desire often argue that sexual desire is socially constructed, a view I explore in Essay 4. There is, however, little agreement surrounding the nature of social constructionism. Various disparate accounts are often not clearly distinguished. Similarly problems are found with Foucault, who fails to support his claim that sexual desire is a social construction. Difficulties also appear in the scripting theory of sexual desire, a theory that is commonly applauded as thoroughgoing a social constructionism. This is because there is much inconsistency involved in the theory's application of theatrical metaphors to everyday life.

I present an alternative phenomenological view that sexual desire has its origin in existential features of human awareness. In this view sexual desire arises simply because we are aware of both our own gender and the genders of others. Here our gender is something that presents itself in awareness as being in need of completion. Sexual desire, then, is the desire for the mutual baring and caressing of bodies, for it is through this baring and caressing we come to experience the completion we yearn for.

There are, however, different degrees of social constructionism about sexual desire. One such degree is the view that the direction or orientation of sexual desire is socially constructed. A well-known account of this view is presented by the social anthropologist Gilbert Herdt. Herdt bases his position on his fieldwork with the Sambia tribe of the Eastern Highlands of Papua New Guinea. Yet a close reading of Herdt's work makes it clear that his data do not support his social constructionist conclusions.

The aspect of Sambia sexual culture on which Herdt focuses is the culturally prescribed period of male homosexuality which takes place prior to the Sambia male's heterosexual marriage. Sambia practice here involves young boys coerced into performing fellatio on older boys. The reason for this is the Sambia belief that young boys need to ingest sperm in order to mature into strong men. Herdt claims that the existence of the prescribed period of homosexual practice followed by heterosexual marriage shows that the direction of sexual desire is socially constructed.

The problem, however, is that nothing in his data suggests that either the younger or older boys engage in the homosexual acts because of homosexual desire. It is well established that people of one sexual orientation can sexually interact and even have orgasms with someone of the undesired gender. They do this through the use of fantasy. Herdt, however, completely ignores this possibility and instead uses biased language to make it look like homosexual desires are behind the behaviour.

In Essay 6 I move from the topic of the direction of sexual desire to that of the amount of sexual desire or its expression in sexual activity. A common idea here is that there such a thing as "too much" sexual activity. Such an idea, I point out, has roots in moral and religious fundamentalism like that displayed by the mediaeval Christian thinker Augustine. I reject this idea by examining a study that claims to have discovered what counts as excessive levels of sexual behaviour. Niklas Långström and R. Karl Hanson, the authors of this study, claim that any rate of sexual behaviour over the 90th percentile of their sample constitutes a disorder.

However, as I show, they fail to demonstrate that the "undesirable features" correlated with high levels of sexual behaviour are in fact a result of the sexual behaviour. Rather it seems that the levels of sexual behaviour in these instances are themselves the results of the undesirable features. Further, high levels of sexual behaviour are only correlated with such features in "impersonal" sex for men, not impersonal sex for women or in "personal" sex for men or women within a romantic relationship. This strongly suggests that there is no such thing as excessive levels of sexual behaviour in itself.

From here I turn the focus to a particular and atypical case of sexual desire, showing how this too is best understood as the desire for mutual baring and caressing. The particular instance I focus on in Essay 7 is a case study of a subject who has age dysphoria, that is a deep desire to be a different age In this case the subject longs to be an infant. This desire is intimately wedded with sexual desires such that the subject is sexually aroused at the idea of being a baby, has masturbates to fantasies about being a baby, and seeks out women sexual partners who will mother him. Here I argue that the subject's age dysphoria is tied to sexual desire because the desire is not simply to be a baby, but rather to be bared and caressed like a baby by a "mummy."

In the final essay I return to the issue of the biological basis of sexual desire. Here, however, my concern is not with biological mechanisms like the ebb and flow of sex hormones, but rather with the evolutionary development of a core sexual feature of our bodies. This is the feature of hairless skin or nakedness. Throughout these essays I have pointed to the desire for mutual baring and caressing. What is bared and caressed is just naked skin. Therefore naked skin is a crucial component in sexual desire. But how is it we came to develop naked skin? This is a significant question because all other primates have thick coats of body hair. So it seems that human beings must have lost their body hair for some evolutionary reason.

In this essay I criticize various theories and present what I call the "naked love theory." This theory locates the origin of human hairlessness in the ancestral mother–infant relationship. In this view, hairlessness is ultimately the adaptive consequence of bipedalism. Because of bipedalism, ancestral infants lost their prehensile feet and thus lost the ability to grasp the mother's fur with their feet, as do other primate infants. Early bipedal mothers were thus under pressure to carry the infant. Therefore infants survived only if mothers had a strong desire to hold them. Because of the pleasure of skin-to-skin contact, the desire to hold the infant would have been stronger in mothers possessing a hairless mutation that enabled them to give birth to hairless infants. The hairlessness that began to appear in this context of maternal selection was, I argue, then reinforced by sexual selection in the male–female sexual relationship. This is because a hairless sexual partner would have enabled the hairless individual to recreate the pleasure of skin-to-skin contact in the mother–infant relationship. This theory then helps to explain the evolutionary origins of romantic love, showing how it is intimately connected to sexual desire.

The ideas in this book were developed in discussions through the years with more people than I would be able to mention here. I owe, however, a special thanks to Gary Heathcote for his helpful comments on Essay 8 and to Elizabeth Edenberg and Ross Hughes for their helpful comments on Essay 1. I should also say that versions of Essays 3 and 4 were previously published as "Sex Hormones and Sexual Desire" and "Social Constructionism and Sexual Desire" in the *Journal for the Theory of Social Behaviour*. Similarly, versions of Essays 5 and 6 were previously published as "Sambia Sexual Culture: Essays from the Field. By Gilbert Herdt," "The Heterosexual/Homosexual Distinction: A Reply to McConaghy," and "No Such Thing as Excessive Levels of Sexual Behavior" in *Archives of Sexual Behavior*. Finally, a version of Essay 8 was previously published as "Naked Love: The Evolution of Human Hairlessness" in *Biological Theory*. I therefore thank the respective publishers Wiley-Blackwell and Springer for permission to reprint this material here.

1
The Meaning of "Gender"

SEX AND GENDER

Human sexuality is intimately tied to our awareness of the features of being a male or female. Yet, despite the significance of sexuality in our lives, the question of what constitutes such features is surrounded by difficulties. One problem has to do with the fact that in English we have two words, namely, "sex" or "gender," which have senses that are plainly used interchangeably but which some people feel refer to different phenomena, or at least which they feel should refer to different phenomena. My feeling is that although there might be a sense in which "gender" refers to phenomena that are often related to but not the same as biological sex, there is also a definite sense in which it is generally accepted as being a synonym for "sex."

There are, of course, different senses of both words, senses in which neither of them refers to biological sex or related phenomena and in which neither of them can be used in place of the other. The word "gender," for example, is also used as a technical term in grammar in a way in which the word "sex" is not. Likewise, the word "sex" is used in ways that the word "gender" is not, as, for example, in the sentence "They had sex two times yesterday." It would make no sense to say, "They had gender two times yesterday."

However, when used in the sense of referring to being a biological male or female, it seems "gender" and "sex" can be and frequently are used synonymously. Thus, someone might ask about the infant's sex or about its gender, or the police might ask about the suspect's sex or about the suspect's gender, or a form may ask us to indicate our sex or to indicate our gender. In each case the terms "sex" and "gender" are being used to refer to the same thing, namely, to a person's maleness or femaleness. A recent example I saw of this synonymy was in the security section of an airport. To the side where searches were conducted a sign said, "Please let us know if you wish to be searched by a person of your own gender." Here the word is referring to the sex of the person to be searched.

Although these sorts of considerations are overtly linguistic considerations about the meanings of terms, they are not solely linguistic. This is because an examination of the language used surrounding a particular phenomenon will often reveal how we understand that phenomenon. Because of this, the discovery of linguistic confusions will also often reveal a confused understanding of the phenomenon that the language is meant to capture. It is in this way that I hope the exploration of the meaning of these terms will help us to get a better understanding of the nature or metaphysics of gender.

Now, the question of what constitutes the sex that both of the terms "gender" and "sex" are here referring to is a complex one. There are, for example, chromosomes, hormones, anatomy, along with other biological features and complex relations between these. However, the decisive features, I would argue, are the genitals. That is, what determines an individual's sex are the genitals the person has. This view, which I have argued for elsewhere and so will not repeat my arguments here, thus implies that a person's gender, in the sense that I am discussing here, is likewise determined by the person's genitals.[1] In other words, if the genitals are what determines sex, and if gender in the sense that I am discussing means the same thing as sex, then the genitals are also what determines gender in this sense. Thus, one is a male because one has male genitals, and one is a female because one has female genitals.

None of this, however, should be taken to imply that there are only two forms of sex or gender. Or, to put it another way, none of this implies that all persons are either male or female. There are, as is well known, persons who have an intersexual condition that renders them neither clearly male nor clearly female. Such a person's intersexual state is determined, significantly enough, by having genitals that are neither clearly male nor clearly female. The genitals of an intersexed person are thus said to be ambiguous. The sex or gender of an intersexed individual can therefore also be seen to be ambiguous.

There are also, however, intersexual conditions where the external genitals are not ambiguous. In such conditions there is rather a lack of consistency between the sex chromosomes, internal anatomy, and the appearance of the external genitals. For example, in the intersexual condition known as androgen insensitivity syndrome, the individual has male sex chromosomes, but, because of a developmental disorder, has female external genitals. Because of their female genitals, persons with this condition will tend to be seen by both others and themselves, as a female. Indeed, an individual with this condition can be unaware that she has the condition and so have no doubts about seeing herself as being fully female. This again shows the importance of the genitals in determining how we think about sex and thus about gender in the sense of "sex." A condition that raises similar questions is that of transsexualism. I will come to this shortly.

Despite the synonymy of the terms "sex," and this sense of "gender" some people have claimed that there is no sense in which they are synonyms. Thus, in a much cited work, Susanne J. Kessler and Wendy McKenna say that, in contrast to the word "sex" which refers to biological features, "the term 'gender' has traditionally been used to designate psychological, social, and cultural aspects of maleness and femaleness."[2] They are thus making a historical claim about how in fact people have used the word "gender"

Their claim, however, does not sit well with the fact that as early as 1783 Hugh Blair, a principle figure in the enlightenment at Edinburgh, stated that "gender, being founded on the distinction of the two sexes, it is plain, that, in a proper sense, it can only find place in the names of living creatures, which admit of the distinction of male and female."[3] Here is a statement by a thinker in the early modern tradition that gender refers to the sex of animals who can be classified as male or female. It is worth noting that the work in which Blair makes this statement was immensely popular and went through 132 editions up to 1911. This use of "gender," differs little, I feel, from its everyday modern usage. It thus seems that, traditionally, there is a clear sense in which the word "gender" refers to sex, and not to ideas like "psychological, social and cultural aspects of maleness and femaleness."

Further, Kessler and McKenna themselves, only a few lines later, call their own claim into question by saying, "gender is a word which, until very recently, was rarely used by people in everyday life, and even in technical writings the two terms are often used interchangeably and confusingly." One cannot help but wonder how a word that only came into everyday use recently, can have a "traditional" use. It might be thought that the traditional use that Kessler and McKenna are referring to is a traditional technical use, rather than traditional everyday use, but Kessler and McKenna themselves exclude this possibility. For they say that even in technical writings the terms in question are frequently used "interchangeably and confusingly." However, the fact that the word "gender" is, even in technical writings, often used interchangeably and confusingly with the word "sex" suggests that the word "gender" does have a sense that is interchangeable with "sex," and that any confusion here is merely the result of a failure to realize this.

It is important to see that I am not here arguing that the traditional use of the term "gender" shows that there is no important distinction between the terms "sex" and "gender." Rather, I am showing that Kessler and McKenna's own historical argument about the traditional use of "gender" is fallacious.

None of this means that the word "gender" refers exclusively to sex, for there has been much scholarly discussion over the last few decades that has focused on the relations between sex and psychological and social elements. In these discussions the term "gender" has begun to acquire a further meaning, a meaning which is said to contain these elements in various ways. But this in no way implies that there is not an important and everyday sense of the word "gender" that is synonymous with the word "sex." Nor does it show that people are somehow wrong to use "gender" in its everyday sense. It does not show, for example, that the airport officials have made a mistake in using the word "gender" to refer to the maleness or femaleness of the person to conduct a personal search.

One response to the awareness that it is acceptable to use "gender" in its normal sense where it means "sex"—a response motivated by the desire that it should not be acceptable—is to argue that a useful distinction can be made by redefining them to refer to separate things. One of the first people to put forward this view was Rhoda Unger. She argues that since there is apparent confusion between the biological and social properties of sex, many problems could be resolved by using the term "gender" to refer to the social properties of sex. She implies that the term "sex" should be used to refer to the biological properties of sex.[4]

More recently, Hillary Lips has given a clearer statement of this view, saying, that for those who followed it, "*sex* was used to refer to a person's biological maleness or femaleness, *gender* to the nonphysiological aspects of being male or female—the cultural expectations for femininity or masculinity."[5] This distinction seemed to be useful, says Lips, because it pointed to the fact that many female–male differences in behaviour are not biologically based. Lips herself does not accept the suggestion, claiming merely that cultural expectations for men and women are not separable from male and female physiology.

Unfortunately, she offers no arguments to support her claim. This is unfortunate because her claim seems obviously false and therefore is in much need of support. Although there are ways in which cultural expectations for men and women are connected to their physiology—a culture, for example, might expect women, but not men, to get pregnant—there are also ways in which culture and physiology are plainly separable. For example, women will normally develop breasts and men will normally produce sperm regardless of whether their culture would expect them to or not.

A more extreme version of the view that cultural expectations for men and women are not separable from male and female physiology is given by Judith Butler. Butler's position, which seems widely popular, is given in her claim that "there is no recourse to a body that has not always already been interpreted by cultural meanings; hence, sex could not qualify as a prediscursive anatomical facticity."[6]

But what does this mean? It sounds like Butler is trying to say we can never know if a particular body is biologically male or female because our perceptions of the sexually determining features of the human body are always interpreted through "cultural meanings."

One need not look too far, however, to see the problems that such an account brings with it. For what this means is that if one were to view a naked man and a naked woman standing beside each other, and even thoroughly examine what one thinks are their physical bodies, one would have no way of knowing which was the biological man and which was the biological woman. For even though one might think one is examining physical bodies, one has no actual knowledge of these bodies and is really just examining "cultural meanings." And because there are no essential relations between a physical body and the "cultural meanings" it has, then a biological man could just as easily have a vaginal examine as a biological woman. This is because the examining gynaecologist has no recourse to a woman's "prediscursive anatomical faciticity," and although the gynaecologist might think she is examining the woman's physical vagina, she is really just examining interpretations of "cultural meanings" (whatever that might mean). Since it is not "anatomical facticity" she is examining, then it is not necessary that the person she is examining has, as a matter of anatomical fact(icity), a vagina. The gynaecologist could therefore just as easily perform a vaginal exam on a biological man (whatever that might mean).

Further, if there is no access to "to a body that has not always already been interpreted by cultural meanings," then not only does sex not qualify as a "prediscursive anatomical facticity," but the body itself does not qualify. Consequently, not only could one not tell the difference between a biological man and a biological woman, but one could not tell the difference between a human body and a lamp post. For unless we have recourse to a human body's prediscursive bodily facticity and a lamp post's prediscursive metallurgical facticity, then in each case all we perceive are cultural meanings, never the actual body or the actual lamp post. And since cultural meanings have no essential connection to the inaccessible thing that they are supposedly meanings about, then we could never tell the difference between such things. In such a situation one might well end up having a conversation with a lamp post while mistakenly thinking it was a person. These considerations should be enough to show the confusion inherent in such a view.

Returning now to the redefinition suggestion, it is clear that this will also generate problems. For to define "gender" exclusively in this way is to try to ride roughshod over a perfectly normal and widely accepted use of the term. We do not, for example, say that a biological male is of the female gender, even if he behaves according to cultural expectations for femininity. For "female gender," in its ordinary usage, means "biological female sex," and a biological male cannot be of the biological female sex. And this remains true,

I should repeat, even though there are intersexual cases in which a person's gender is ambiguous. For in such cases we do not have a man who is also a biological female, or a woman who is also a biological male. Rather, what we have is a person whose gender is ambiguous and thus neither fully a biological male nor fully a biological female. This is what the term "intersexual" means. Such a person may identify with being a man or a woman, but that is another matter and one that I will come to shortly.

Further, as Blair points out, the term "gender" here is applicable not just to human beings, but to any living creatures which admit of the distinction between male and female. Consequently, to redefine gender to mean exclusively cultural expectations for femininity or masculinity would be to make it inapplicable to non-human animals. Thus, unless one wants to allow that cows and bulls have cultural expectations for femininity or masculinity, we would no longer be able to refer to the gender of oxen.

Moreover, although it is clearly useful to make a distinction between biological maleness or femaleness and cultural expectations for masculinity and femininity, it seems not useful to try to force the word "gender" to stand exclusively for the cultural expectations half of the distinction.

One reason for this is that the meaning of a word cannot be legislated. Consequently, even if a group of scholars were to proclaim that the word "gender" was from now on exclusively to mean "expectations for femininity or masculinity," it is doubtful that this would be enough to make the hundreds of millions of other English language users toe the line. That is, a large majority of people would probably continue to use the word in its established way. Even the scholars themselves would not be immune from inadvertently using the word in the established way. This could lead to all sorts of misunderstandings. For example, someone who is discussing sex might, because of the new exclusive definition, begin to think that he or she was instead discussing cultural expectations for femininity or masculinity. A good instance of this can already be seen in Lynn Chancer and Beverly Watkins' account of the definition of gender. According to these scholars,

> Many introductory Women Studies classes begin with a simple but solid sociological approach, differentiating "sex" and "gender" to clarify the meaning of each. "Sex" is said to refer primarily to anatomical distinctions between women and men at birth; it is a term of biology, of physiology, that is arguably neutral . . . Gender, on the other hand refers to interpretations that have been socially constructed to skew the arguably "neutral" facts of gender in one evaluative direction or another.[7]

They then say that the most likely thing that people ask about when they hear a baby has been born is not how much it weighs or if it is healthy, but rather they will ask if it is a boy or a girl. "This suggests," they tell us, "that gender takes on . . . a 'primary status'; it trumps all other possible observations one could make about a given social phenomenon."[8]

Here we see that despite their using the "simple but solid" approach of defining "sex" to refer to anatomy and "gender" to refer to socially constructed interpretations, Chancer and Watkins themselves confuse the two. When people ask about whether an infant is a boy or a girl, they are asking a biological question, just as asking about the weight or health of the infant is to ask biological questions. Thus this question, according to their own definition, is a question about the infant's sex, not about its gender. But if the question is about sex, why do they say the fact that people ask this question suggests that "gender" takes on a primary status? On Chancer and Watkins' own account, gender has nothing to do with this question. And why do they then state that the question trumps all other observations that could be made about a "social phenomenon?" The question about the infant's sex is about a biological phenomenon, not a social phenomenon or socially constructed interpretations. Chancer and Watkins have started out discussing sex but ended up thinking they were instead discussing cultural expectations for femininity or masculinity. One can only have sympathy for the students in the courses using this simple but solid approach.

In the same way, someone who starts using "gender" to refer exclusively to cultural expectations for femininity or masculinity might, because of the prevalence of the established meaning, get the mistaken idea that discussions about cultural expectations for femininity or masculinity somehow have implications about sex.

Something like this, I suspect, is what is already going on with the popular proclamation that gender is culturally constructed. This assertion is often made as though it were supposed to be saying something about gender in the ordinary sense of male or female, that is, as though it were saying that maleness and femaleness are culturally constructed. But when one reads further it usually becomes clear that "gender" is here being understood to mean something like cultural expectations for masculinity and femininity. But if this is what is going on, then the assertion that gender is culturally constructed is little more than a tautology. For here "gender" just means "cultural expectations for femininity or masculinity." Thus, saying that gender is culturally constructed is the same as saying that the cultural expectations for femininity or masculinity are culturally constructed, which says next to nothing.

This assertion about gender and cultural construction is one that seems to have its roots in a misunderstanding of Simon de Beauvoir's celebrated claim that "one is not born, but rather becomes a woman." The problem appears to be that many people have taken this claim literally rather than seeing it within its context. But if one wants to takes this claim literally, then it too is a tautology. Of course one is not born a woman (*femme* in Beauvoir's French), for a woman is, by definition, an adult female, and adults are, by definition, not born: only infants are born. Not noticing this tautology, and taking it slightly less literally, one might be led to think Beauvoir is saying that a person becomes a woman through some form of social construction, not through biology, that is, through birth.

Reading further, however, makes it clear that Beauvoir does not mean this to be taken literally in either way. For in the very next line what she says is that it is culture or "civilization as a whole," as she puts it, that "determines the figure that the human female presents in society."[9] So what Beauvoir is claiming here is not that culture constructs or civilization determines whether someone is a woman—that is, an adult of the female gender—but rather that culture determines the figure the human female presents in society. In other words, a person of the female gender is female regardless of what culture does. Culture's role is merely to determine how someone who is already female presents herself as a female to society.

GENDER IDENTITY

It is significant to note that the way in which someone presents himself or herself to society as either a male or female is something that is often referred to as a gender or sex role. These terms are also frequently used to refer to cultural expectations for masculinity and femininity. Such expectations are expectations for men and women to engage in the roles or behaviours that a culture traditionally associates with men or women. This is another reason why it seems unhelpful to try to redefine gender to mean such expectations. For with the term "gender role" we already have such a term. It is also a useful term because, in containing the term "gender," it shows clearly that the idea of a gender role is different from, though related to, the idea of gender. That is, cultural expectations for masculinity and femininity are different from, though related to, gender.

Nevertheless, various scholars have argued not just that gender is the same thing as such expectations, but that gender also contains the idea of gender identity. There is, however, a lack of clarity attending this further notion. As Anne Lawrence puts it, gender identity is "a slippery, imprecisely defined concept with a variety of possible meanings."[10] It is also, I would add, unclear just how it is supposed to be related to gender. For example, in one widely accepted account of gender identity, John Money and Anke A. Ehrhardt define it as "the sameness, unity, and persistence of one's individuality as male, female or ambivalent, in greater or lesser degree, especially as it is experienced in self-awareness and behavior; gender identity is the private experience of gender role, and gender role is the public expression of gender identity."[11]

But this is problematic on several points. First, one wants to ask: what does it mean to speak about one's "individuality as male, female or ambivalent?" Were we to say, for example, that someone has "individuality" as an artist it would normally be understood to mean that she is distinct from other artists or has her own special artistic style. But this does not seem to be what Money and Ehrhardt want to say about individuality as a male, female, or ambivalent. For they are not speaking of anyone in particular or saying that any particular person has his or her own distinctiveness as male, female, or ambivalent. Rather, they seem to be giving a general definition.

But then what could they mean? One possible answer is that here "individuality as a male, female, or ambivalent" simply refers to the fact of being male, female, or ambivalent. But the fact of being a male or a female is quite a different sort of fact from the fact of being ambivalent. For being male or female does not have much to do with being in a specific psychological state: "Is it a boy or a girl?" or "Was the suspect a man or woman?" hardly seem to be questions about an infant's or suspect's specific psychological state. Being ambivalent, however, is a psychological state. That is, to be ambivalent is to be in a state of conflicting emotions or thoughts over something. In Money and Ehrhardt's definition these conflicting emotions are, I suppose, meant to be about being male or female. Thus, a male who has conflicting emotions about being a male might be said to be ambivalent about being a male.

But if this is how the idea of ambivalence is here to be understood, then obviously it is not something independent from being male or female. On the contrary, it relies on the idea that one is a male or female in the first place. For the only way that one can be ambivalent about being a male is if one is a male. Consequently, it is unclear why Money and Ehrhardt refer to ambivalence in their definition, disjoining it from male and female as if it represented a third and distinct category. Here they seem to be confusing the fact of being male or female with feelings about being male or female.

It might be thought that the way out of this comes in the next part of the definition where they say that gender identity refers to this individuality "especially as it is experienced in self-awareness and behavior," for here they are no longer referring merely to the fact of being male or female but also to the experience of this fact. Although this part of the definition now seems to enable us to distinguish gender identity from gender, it also means that gender identity is more complex than gender itself. In this case gender identity is made up of both gender (the fact of being male or female) and the experience of that fact. Perhaps here is where the idea of ambivalence is meant to fit in. Consequently, far from helping to explain gender, gender identity presupposes it.

Things become even more confused when in the final part of the definition we are told that "gender identity is the private experience of gender role, and gender role is the public expression of gender identity." Here gender identity is not even something that has "especially" to do with experience, but is now said to be wholly a matter of private experience. And, to make matters worse, the fact of being male, female, or ambivalent completely drops out of the definition and it is now asserted that gender identity is the experience of one's "gender role."

Now, although the concept of gender role is, as I said, usually taken to refer to behaviour roles that a culture traditionally associates with each gender, here it is said to be a public expression of a private experience, a definition that makes no reference to cultural roles and that clearly need make no such reference. For one may publicly express the private experience of one's gender in a way that has nothing to do with culturally prescribed roles. But this leaves us with little more than a circular definition: to understand what gender role is we must first understand what gender identity is, but to understand what gender identity is we must first understand what gender role is.

A way around this problem might seem to be found in Butler's account of gender identity. This is because Butler rejects the distinction between gender role and gender identity. Reformulating Nietzsche's claim that there is no doer behind the doing, Butler asserts, "There is no gender identity behind the expressions of gender; that identity is performatively constituted by the very 'expressions' that are said to be its results."[12] Nietzsche's claim, of course, offers no support for Butler's. This is because Nietzsche assertion is a rejection the idea of a substantial self that operates as a cause behind actions and experiences. He is not rejecting the idea of experience itself. Butler, however, seems to be rejecting the idea of the experience of identity. What she appears to be saying is that gender identity has nothing to do with private experiences of public expressions, rather it simply is the expressions.

This account, unfortunately, faces the same difficulties as does the philosophical behaviourism on which it is based. The behaviourist thesis is that there are no conscious experiences behind the behavioural expressions of those states and, consequently, that conscious experiences are really just behaviour. The problem with this is that people can easily pretend to be in a specific conscious state. For example, someone who is in pain can pretend not to be in pain by choosing not to display any pain behaviour. Behaviourists deal with this problem by arguing that dispositions to show the behaviour in the appropriate circumstances, and not just actual behaviour, are also relevant. Consequently, even though someone in pain can pretend not to be, she still has the disposition to show pain behaviour when, for example, she has no reasons to keep up the pretence.

Few people, however, especially someone in pain, seem convinced by such an account. For conscious experiences present themselves to us in ways that are plainly more than behaviour. Intense pain has a raw horribleness to it that has little essential connection to the behaviour that expresses it or dispositions to express it.

The same could be said about this view of gender identity. A person can easily have the private experience of identifying with one gender and yet only express the behaviour of the other gender. Perhaps he or she has deep conflicts, embarrassment, or guilt over the private experience and so seeks to keep it hidden. On this account one would have to say that a woman, for example, who expresses only feminine behaviour but has the private experience of strongly identifying with being a man, nevertheless has a feminine gender identity. This leads to the peculiar state of affairs where a person's gender identity is always, by definition, congruent with his or her behaviour.

As a consequence, the idea of gender identity can no longer be used to explain the idea of gender dysphoria or the state of being intensely unhappy with one's sex. Or rather, it can only be used to explain those instances where someone's public expression of masculinity or femininity is congruent with his or her sex. Or it might be felt suitable for a woman who likes to dress and act masculine or a man who likes to dress and act feminine. For such an account still allows them to assert they have a cross-gender identity. But in cases of a hidden gender identity like the one just mentioned—where the person keeps her sense of being a different sex private—then there is no incongruence. Yet in such cases there clearly is something could be called gender dysphoria, an experiential state which can be a crucial component of transsexualism. But it is unclear how gender dysphoria here could then be explained.

A more promising account is given by Richard F. Docter. According to Docter, gender identity can be thought of as

> the organized perceptions of oneself as masculine or feminine. A sense of gender identity is therefore a totally subjective-experiential matter. What counts is how one perceives oneself and this is a phenomenological matter. Although gender identity may be inferred from behaviour, to some extent, this is not always the case. It is useful to think of gender identity as multidimensional—as encompassing potential feelings and evaluations having both masculine and feminine qualities rather than as a point along a gender continuum.[13]

The advances of this account over both Money and Ehrhardt's and Butler's are obvious. First, Docter does not confuse notions about having a gender with the private experience of having a gender. Secondly, he makes it clear that gender identity is an experiential matter. Thirdly, and connected with this, in his definition he avoids using the terms "male" and "female" and refers instead to "masculine" and "feminine."Although these terms also have a vagueness about them, at least it is plain that they do not necessarily refer to the male and female genders. For it is no contradiction to say that a person of the male gender experiences himself as feminine or a person of the female gender experiences herself as masculine. Using these terms allows Docter to keep his account consistently within the experiential realm. Fourthly, and consistent with his experiential approach, Docter allows that a person's gender identity might not be expressed in his or her public behaviour. That is, a male, for example, might feel himself to be feminine, but nevertheless, and for any number of reasons, continue to behave in a masculine way. Such a person could be said to have a feminine gender identity even though he was of the male gender and displayed masculine behaviour. Further, on this account it is possible for a male or female to have a mixed sense of femininity and masculinity.

With this, however, it is now evident that gender identity has little to do with a person's actual gender. That is, having a specific gender identity—a subjective perception of oneself as masculine or feminine—has no bearing on whether one is male or female.

GENDER AND TRANSSEXUALISM

Although this conclusion seems obvious, it might be felt that it is challenged by the condition of transsexualism. Although there is some disagreement what the term refers to, the American Psychological Association says it is a condition that fits within the broader category of transgenderism. It suggests that while "transgenderism" refers to a broad range of gender non-conformity, "the term *transsexual* refers to people whose gender identity is different from their assigned sex. Often, transsexual people alter or wish to alter their bodies through hormones, surgery, and other means to make their bodies as congruent as possible with their gender identities."[14]

This account suggests why transsexualism might challenge the idea gender identity has little to do with a person's actual gender. For in many cases it is more than mere subjective perception. In such cases it also involves changes, or at least persistent desires for changes, to the transsexual's biology and sexual anatomy.

There are, however, problems with this view. Not only does it fail to mention gender dysphoria, which is often seen to be part of the transsexual condition, but also the sense of incongruent identity mentioned seems not to be universally held or at least not universally deep-rooted among transsexuals. For example, in the case of male-to-female transsexuals—biological men who desire to be women—there are those who maintain their male sense of identity but are sexually aroused by the idea of having a female body. Such men are typically sexually attracted to women and are thus heterosexual relative to natal sex. If there is a sense of feminine gender identity in such cases, Lawrence, herself a transsexual, argues that it is more of an epiphenomenon than a deep-rooted sense of identity. This form of transsexualism, which is called autogynephilia[15] and means "love of oneself as a woman," is characterized by Lawrence as "men trapped in men's bodies."[16]

This suggests that that transsexuals are not exclusively "people whose gender identity is different from their assigned sex." And of course, the American Psychological Association is not saying that *all* transsexual people who wish to thus alter their bodies in this way are doing so because of their gender identities. But the fact that it omits any reference to other motivations does imply that it sees it as being the only reason.

With male-to-female transsexuals who are homosexual relative to natal sex, gender identity seems to play more of a role. The same seems to be true of female-to-male transsexuals, the majority of whom seem to be homosexual relative to natal sex, though there is less evidence here.[17] With these transsexuals cross-gender behaviour and identification tends to appear earlier in life. However, even in these cases it is not at all clear why merely identifying with another gender should be enough to make that person into the gender he or she identifies with. We do not accept, for example, that an emaciated person with an anorexic condition is obese simply because she identifies with being obese or that an adult who identifies with being an infant is thereby an infant.

It is significant to note that in this last-mentioned case, which I will discuss in Essay 6, the individual suffers from what I call age dysphoria, a condition that has parallels to gender dysphoria. In gender dysphoria, the individual is deeply unhappy with being the gender he or she is, longs to be the other gender, and even identifies with the other gender. In age dysphoria, the individual is deeply unhappy with being the age he or she is, longs to be another age, typically that of a child, and even identifies with being the age that he or she longs to be. Few people, however, seem willing to accept that an adult who has this sense of identity with an infant is thereby a real infant.

Or, to go one step further, consider the case of people known as "otherkins" who deeply identify with being a particular animal. Many people with this condition say their identification is merely "spiritual," but some experience it as an actual identity. Such persons are aware that they have a human body but frequently feel themselves to be, say, "a fox trapped in a human body." Thus, here we have "species dysphoria" and "species identity" with another species. In some cases otherkins will even have surgery in an attempt to resemble more closely the animal they identify with.[18] Even so, it seems few people would be willing to accept such a person really is, say, a fox, bat, or horse. But if simply identifying with a particular animal is not enough to make a person into the animal, why should simply identifying with a female be enough to make a person into a female?

One argument here, given by Talia Mae Bettcher, is that it all depends on the context or the larger question of the gendered vision of the world we are committed to. Thus, if we are committed to the context in which someone who identifies as a woman is a woman, despite the fact that the person has a male body and genitals, then that person is a woman.

But as Bettcher herself puts it, this sounds much like saying "*Of course* you're a teapot, if by 'teapot' we mean 'human being.' And *of course* you're a woman, if by 'woman' we mean 'man who lives as a woman.'" Although such claims seem little more than a semantic sleight of hand, Bettcher assures us that this move "is no verbal trick but tracks a difference between cultural practices of gender and the relation of these practices to the interpretation of the body and self-presentation."[19]

What this line of argument comes down to, it seems, is a contextually or culturally relative view of truth. It is much the same argument that Peter Winch and others use to justify religious and superstitious claims.[20] According to this view, religious claims, like "God exists" or superstitious claims like "Witchcraft made me do it" can only be said to be true or false when assessed from within the culture in which the claims are made. Likewise, claims such as "I am a woman" can only be said to be true or false when assessed from within the culture (or sub-culture) in which they are made.

This view, however, is plagued with difficulties. What, for example, happens when opposing views are held within the same culture? In Western culture there are those who believe that God exists and those who do not believe that God exists. So how do we assess the truth of such a claim from within our culture? The answer to this is exceedingly unclear. Likewise, in "trans-culture," as Bettcher calls it, there are transsexuals who believe that male-to-female transsexuals are real women and there are male-to-female transsexuals who do not believe this. For example, Jenny Roberts, a male-to-female transsexual, says, "As M to F transsexuals, we can never be real women. However distasteful we may find it, and however hard some transsexuals may argue against it, the inescapable fact is that we've grown up with gender privilege . . . We don't know what it's like to grow up as a girl in a male dominated society, we'll never experience women's puberty and menopause, we can't conjure up the social experience of growing up female."[21] Here too, then, there is a similar problem of deciding on the truth of the claim that male-to-female transsexuals are women.

However, the more serious difficulty with this sort of relativism is that it ultimately contradicts itself. For to claim that all truth is relative to the culture or context in which the truth claims are made is to assert something that is supposed to be universally true independently of any cultural context. That is, it is on par with saying, "It is a universal truth that there is no such thing as universal truth," which is a contradiction.

Transsexualism presents more of a challenge, it would seem, in those cases where there are actual hormonal and surgical alterations to the transsexual's biology and sexual anatomy. For in such cases the genitals of the transsexual can come to resemble the genitals of the gender the transsexual identifies with or desires to be. And the genitals, as I have argued elsewhere, are the basis of gender. Here, then, the question becomes "Are male genitals that have been surgically reconstructed to resemble female genitals actual female genitals, or are they merely partial male genitals that have been surgically reshaped? Or are they even genitals at all?" The way one answers this question would seem to be based on how much importance one places on the history or temporal development of the genitals in question.

Taking one position it could be argued that the essential thing is the resemblance the genitals have to female genitals, not their development. But one could reject this view. In the quote just given, for example, Roberts argues for the importance of social and biological development in determining whether someone is a woman. Implicit in this view is the idea of the importance of the biological development of the genitals. Focusing on just this point one could argue that male genitals that have been surgically reconstructed to resemble female genitals are not female genitals. For female genitals cannot once have been male genitals.

Adjudicating between these views, however, is not easy. This is because in one way the history of an object might have little bearing on its nature. One could imagine, for example, a science-fiction-like case in which a perfectly functioning and full-grown human being with a female body and genitals was suddenly created out of various molecules by an advanced machine. In such an instance the individual would, simply by virtue of her body, have a strong claim to being a woman. It is in this sort of case the resemblance argument would seem to be the decisive criterion.

But this is not what happens with the sex reassignment surgery undergone by a transsexual. In this case it is a pre-existing person of one gender who has his or her genitals surgically altered to resemble the genitals of the other gender. Here there is a bodily continuity that ties together the pre- and post-operative body. Because of this bodily continuity the male-to-female transsexual's body is the body of, as Roberts puts it, an "ex-man." And, therefore the genitals are "ex-male" genitals. This fact seems to weaken the claim that they are real female genitals, and therefore that the bearer of the genitals is a real female. Or at least it creates a doubt that is not present in the case of a biological female. Nevertheless, even if one wants to accept that the transsexual's post-operative genitals are real genitals of the other gender, and therefore the post-operative transsexual is real member of the other gender, then this would also prove my point, namely, that it is the genitals and not gender identity that are the bases of gender.

One of the concerns about entertaining the conclusion that the transsexual might not really be a member of the gender he or she desires to be is that some people feel it implies that a transsexual should not be afforded the full rights of that gender. Thus, someone might feel that the fact that a male-to-female transsexual is not a real woman implies that she should not be allowed to use women's toilets, while also legitimating other forms of discrimination.

This of course is an ethical or political concern rather than linguistic or metaphysical one, and so is not a relevant critique of the arguments I have made. Nevertheless, I hasten to point out that there is no reason why there should be any such implication. The whole idea of specific gender rights or of distinct men's and women's toilets, for example, is an anachronism tied to traditional gender segregation and stereotypes that serves no good purpose anyway. In the Scandinavian university where I teach there are no distinct men's and women's toilets. Further, I can see no reason why a person's gender should have any legal or discriminatory implications. And just as there is no good reason why a person's race should be mentioned on his or her birth certificate or passport, so there is no good reason why a person's gender need be mentioned. Therefore, rather than argue that transsexuals should be able to have their gender changed on their birth certificate—which implies there is some good reason for having gender noted on a birth certificate—the real non-discriminatory position would be to argue that gender has no place on *anyone's* birth certificate.

It is worthwhile to note here that those who argue that male-to-female transsexuals, but not other biological men, should be allowed into women's toilets are actually working to support gender stereotypes and a gender-segregated society. And the same is true for those who demand that female-to-male transsexuals should have access to men's toilets or facilities, but at the same time feel that other biological women should not have such access. In these cases it seems that the person holding such a position is actually happy with gender stereotypes and segregation. It is just that he or she wants transsexuals to be stereotyped and segregated with the gender they desire to be.

The conclusion is then that transsexualism does not represent a problem for the view that gender in its everyday sense of sex has nothing to do with gender identity. Nor does it show that gender in the same sense means something other than sex or that gender is not based on the genitals. There is a more specialized uncommon sense of gender which means something like cultural expectations for masculinity and femininity, but this does not show that gender in its normal sense has anything to do with such expectations.

2
The Erotic Meaning of the Sexual Positions

THE SEXUAL POSITIONS

That gender plays a foundational role in human existence is obvious to anyone who cares to observe how people interact with each other. In all cultures the gender that a person has will deeply affect how that person understands himself or herself and how other people relate to that person. But why should this be the case? Why should someone's gender be of such vast importance to both the person herself and to other people? The answer, it seems, is not because of any essential property of gender itself, but rather because of gender's central place in both sexual desire and sexual interaction. This is because it is another person's gender that constitutes a core element in our desire to interact sexually with that person. For the heterosexual person it is the opposite gender that plays this role, while for the homosexual person it is the same gender. For the bisexual person both genders play this role.

The question of how exactly gender does this is something I shall explore in Essay 4. For now what I want to look at is the sexual interaction itself, or rather a principal feature of sexual interaction. This is the feature of the sexual position. This is a principal feature because when people engage in sexual interaction each of them must necessarily place himself or herself in a physical position that relates to his or her partner's physical position. My interest, however, is not so much the physical positions themselves, but rather the meanings we attribute to them. For it is in the erotic meanings, as I shall call them, that we can see the object of sexual desire and thus the purpose of sexual interaction when engaged in because of such desire.

What then is a sexual position? Although, as just mentioned, it is a position used in sexual interaction, in its more common use "sexual position" or "sex position" refers more specifically to a position used by two persons during sexual intercourse. This is why sexual positions are also sometimes referred to as coital or intercourse positions. There are of course numerous forms of sexual interaction that do not involve coitus, both heterosexual and homosexual, and each of these will also involve a sexual position. Also, there are sexual positions that involve more than two people. For three or four people can just as easily have sex as two people. However, because of space considerations I will focus on the two-person intercourse positions. It is also the positions for sexual intercourse that have received most attention in the sexological literature. Much of the discussion, though, will also be relevant to other forms of sexual interaction.

One of the fascinating things about human sexual intercourse is that there are several such positions that can be used. This stands in strong contrast to non-human animals who tend to use only one position. For example, in *The Mirror of Coitus*, a Spanish sex manual dating from the 15th century, five main positions with 26 variants are given.

But why is it there are several positions? Unfortunately, *The Mirror of Coitus* gives no reason but simply lists them. One common reply, however, is that the existence of different positions enables people to have variety in their sex life. As one account of the different sexual positions puts it, with "that need to have sex comes the urge to have a bit of variety. Fortunately, there are plenty of different configurations you and your partner can try out."[1] Yet despite the wide variety of positions available it seems that people tend to alternate between two to three different positions.[2] If variety were the principal reason, then it would seem that people would be using much more than two or three positions.

Another view is that different positions contain certain physical qualities that enable people to engage in various degrees of physical control or exertion during sexual intercourse. This seems to be the view that is often put forward in human sexuality textbooks. Thus, in university textbooks meant for courses with titles like "human sexuality" or "the psychology of human sexuality" a list of the various sexual positions—supplemented with drawings—is often given. In one such textbook four primary positions (along with minor variations) are given. These are the man-on-top position (the man and woman lying face to face with the woman on her back), the woman-on-top position (both lying face to face, or the woman sitting, with the man on his back), the lateral-entry position (both lying on one side and facing each other), and the rear-entry position (the woman on her hands and knees with the man kneeling behind her).

This same textbook says, "In the woman-on-top intercourse position, the female can control the angle, rate, and depth of penile penetration." It is further said that, in this position, when the woman is sitting, both partners' hands are free to stimulate each other. We are also told that "In the lateral-entry position, or side-to-side intercourse, neither partner supports their body weight. During pregnancy, illness, or convalescence this alignment is more comfortable and less strenuous than many other intercourse positions."[3]

All of this is of course true. The problem, however, is that the discussion makes it sound like these simple physical qualities, detached from any meaning they might have, are the only or at least the main reasons for choosing one position over the others. Yet if one considers the sexual positions it should be obvious that these sorts of qualities are but minor elements when seen in light of the meanings that the qualities have for people in a sexual encounter. But what are these meanings?

One such meaning, which obviously plays a role in the choice of positions, is what might be called their interpersonal-orientation meaning. This is something that is suggested by William Simon and John H. Gagnon in their "scripting theory" view of human sexuality, which I examine more fully in Essay 4.[4] According to this view, the primary role of the sexual positions is to express or communicate various interpersonal orientations or attitudes. Thus, in the man-on-top position it might be felt that the man primarily expresses his dominance over the woman and the woman, by being on the bottom, primarily expresses her submission to the man. Simon de Beauvoir, for example, refers to the man-on-top position as the "posture of defeat" for the woman.[5]

This, however, should not be interpreted as saying that each sexual position carries a definite or intrinsic interpersonal-orientation meaning, that it will always mean the same thing to everyone who uses it, or even that it will always mean the same thing to the same person. The meaning here will depend on how the participant chooses, for whatever reason, to perceive the interaction. Thus, rather than seeing the man-on-top position as an expression of her own submission, a woman might see the opening of her legs in this position as carrying the meaning of giving, acceptance, or caring. Similarly, rather than perceiving this position as being a form of dominance, the man might see his being on top of the woman as being an expression of his being nurtured by the woman, much as an infant is nurtured while lying on the breast of its mother.

Therefore, interpersonal-orientation meanings are what the individual participant attributes to the sexual position as an interpersonal orientation towards his or her partner. They are not inherent in the interaction but are rather individual interpretations that can vary according to the individual doing the interpretation.

Clearly, these sorts of meanings are present in the various sexual positions. But in themselves such meanings are not essentially sexual or erotic. They make reference to interpersonal attitudes that, in addition to appearing in sexual interactions, can also exist in numerous expressions that have little relation to sexual interaction. Consequently, they convey different ways in which one person can relate to another even without the persons engaging in a sexual position. That is, one person can related to another in a dominant, submissive, giving, or nurturing manner without sexually interacting with that person. A sexual position, however, if done for sexual reasons, is an interaction that would express a meaning beyond these purely interpersonal-orientation meanings. That is, it would also express an erotic meaning. (The term "erotic" is perhaps better here that the term "sexual," since it seems to carry the connotation of desire in a way "sexual" does not.)

THE IDEA OF AN EROTIC MEANING

But how does one distinguish between a person engaging in a sexual position for sexual reasons and a person engaging in a sexual position for the purpose of expressing a non-erotic, interpersonal-orientation meaning? One way of doing this is to see that if a person uses a particular sexual position solely for the purpose of expressing an interpersonal-orientation meaning, then obviously the position lacks or at least has little erotic meaning for that person.

It is important to note, however, that there is nothing in the nature of a sexual position that implies it must have only one sort of meaning for the person involved. In other words, a sexual position may have both interpersonal-orientation and erotic meanings. A person may, for example, be using a particular position to express both a non-erotic, interpersonal-orientation meaning like submission and also an erotic meaning. Indeed, it is likely that most sexual positions carry an array of meanings, both erotic and non-erotic, for the participants. To discover the erotic meaning of the position, then, one must be able to disengage the non-erotic meanings from the erotic meaning.

But to do this, one must first be clear about what it is that enables a sexual position to express an erotic meaning. One way of achieving this is to try to locate the sexual element that is absent when a sexual position is engaged in for the purpose of expressing a non-erotic meaning. Thus, if we consider a man who is, for example, engaging in the man-on-top position primarily for the purpose of putting the woman in the "posture of defeat," what is conspicuously absent from or only minimally present in this interaction is the man's sexual desire. That is, the desire that has led him to choose this position is primarily the desire for expressing dominance. The erotic meaning of a sexual position, then, would be present when the desire that has led a person to choose the position is primarily sexual desire or, in other words, the desire for sexual interaction for its own sake.[6]

As I shall argue in the next essay, the object of sexual desire is the mutual baring and caressing of naked bodies. Consequently, sexual interaction for its own sake is sexual interaction engaged in for the purpose of a mutual baring and caressing of naked bodies. Now, although this enables one to distinguish between instances of the sexual positions that have erotic meaning and those that do not, it does not enable one to distinguish between the erotic meanings that attend the different sexual positions. Distinguishing between the non-erotic meanings here is easy enough because in each case there is a different desire that leads to the adoption of the position. Thus, in order to express hostility, the participant engages in a position that the participant feels best expresses hostility, while in order to express acceptance the participant uses a position that he or she feels best expresses acceptance. The positions carry their different meanings according to the different desires that lie behind their adoption. But in the case of the erotic meanings of the different positions, it seems that in each instance it is the same desire, namely sexual desire, that lies behind the use of each position. So how is it then that the different meanings are attached to the different positions?

Various answers here are possible. One such answer is to reject the idea that the different positions have different erotic meanings. One could claim that once the non-erotic meanings are removed the different sexual positions essentially express the same meaning, which is, it could be argued, simply the desire for sexual interaction. In order to get specific sexual positions (that is, types of sexual activity) desired, one must bring in other non-sexual desires, such as the desires for dominance, submission, acceptance, privacy, and so on. Once these desires are brought into the picture, then and only then can the different positions be seen to have different meanings. These different meanings are interpersonal-orientation meanings.

Another possible answer is to claim that once the interpersonal-orientation meanings are removed, all one is left with are the physical qualities of each position. In this case, one has the freedom of movement for the woman in the woman-on-top position, the ease and non-exertion for both partners in the side-by-side position, the stimulating of the woman's posterior vaginal wall in the rear-entry position, and so on. These physical qualities, it could then be argued, are all that remain once the interpersonal-orientation meanings are removed. As a result it is these qualities alone that constitute the reason for engaging in one position rather than another.

The problem with both these replies is that they fail to account for the sexual dimension of the sexual positions. This dimension, I want to argue, is what gives the sexual positions, indeed all sexual interactions, their erotic or sexually exciting features. This dimension is not present in the purely interpersonal-orientation or the purely physical qualities of freedom of movement, degree of exertion, or some such thing. Consequently, if a sexual position has an erotic meaning, then that meaning must be derived from something other than an interpersonal orientation or the physical qualities just mentioned.

EROTIC MEANING IN THE *KĀMA SŪTRA*

One way to locate the erotic meanings of the sexual positions is suggested by a discussion of these positions in the *Kāma Sūtra*. The *Kāma Sūtra* is an ancient Indian treatise on various aspects of romantic love and sexuality. In this book the author, Vātsyāyana, discusses the different aspects and techniques of sexual interaction. Like *The Mirror of Coitus* he also lists different sexual positions. And like modern sexuality text books he is also interested in the physical features of the sexual positions. His main concern here, however, is in having partners with discrepant sizes of genitals achieve a harmonious joining in sexual intercourse. He thus describes positions in which a woman with a shallow vagina can accommodate a man with a large penis, a man with a small penis can adequately penetrate a woman with a deep vagina, and so on.

However, in addition to both listing sexual positions and the physical considerations, he also describes various positions in terms of other meanings, meanings that do not seem to be primarily ones of interpersonal orientation in the senses just mentioned.

Consider Vātsyāyana's following description:

> Four embraces are used while making love: the 'twining vine', 'climbing the tree', 'rice-and-sesame', and 'milk and water'. As a vine twines around a great dammar tree, so she twines around him and bends his face down to her to kiss him. Or, raising it up again, she pants gently, rests on him, and gazes at him with love for a while. This is the 'twining vine'. She steps on his foot with her foot, places her other foot on his thigh or wraps her leg around him, with one arm gripping his back and the other bending down his shoulder, and panting gently, moaning a little, she tries to climb him to kiss him. This is called 'climbing the tree'. These two embraces are done standing up. Lying on a bed, their thighs entangled and arms entangled, they embrace so tightly that they seem to be wrestling against one another. This is 'rice-and-sesame'. Blind with passion, oblivious to pain or injury, they embrace as if they would enter one another; she may be on his lap, seated facing him, or on a bed. This is called 'milk-and-water.'[7]

To see what is going on here, it is important to note two basic features of this description. First, each position described is given a descriptive metaphorical name and, secondly, the descriptions represent a progression. That is, Vātsyāyana is not just randomly listing different positions, but is placing them in a definite order.

But what is the nature of the progression? The answer to this is given by comparing the different metaphors. Thus in each metaphor two things are referred to which are blended together in various degrees. In the first position the metaphor is of a vine and something it twines around, in the second it is of a tree and something that climbs it, in the third it is of rice and sesame, and in the fourth it is of milk and water.

What is immediately evident here is that, for the most part, each subsequent metaphor represents a higher degree of blending of the two elements than the previous metaphor. The reason I say "for the most part" is because it is perhaps not so evident that a vine which twines around a tree is less blended with the tree than is something that climbs the tree. However, if we compare a situation in which a vine merely twins around a tree with one in which the vine both twines around and climbs the tree, then it is evident that in the second situation the vine is more blended with the tree than it is in the second. Of course, Vātsyāyana does not mention a vine in the second metaphor, but the fact that he refers to the woman and man as a vine and tree in the first metaphor, and the man as a tree in the second metaphor, suggests that here too the woman—who is climbing the tree—plays the role of the vine.

In the third metaphor the two elements, rice and sesame, are even more blended than in the case of the vine and tree. Here the grains of rice and sesame seeds, when they are mixed, are scattered throughout each other. They are, however, still discernible beside each other. But with water and milk, the fourth metaphor, the mixing is such that the two elements have lost their distinctness and are here no longer discernible as independent entities. Here the two elements are fully blended.

It is evident, therefore, that Vātsyāyana wants to say the same thing about the sexual positions that each metaphor is used to describe. That is, he wants to say that each subsequent position he describes involves a higher degree of blending of the man and woman, both physically and experientially. In the first position the woman twines around the man and bends his face down to kiss him while gently panting or she rests on him while gazing at him. This resting on him is the first step in physical and experiential closeness. Gazing at him is the act of visually penetrating him while having him visually penetrate her. It can be seen as the visual equivalent of mutual physical penetration. Her panting is not only a sign of her sexual excitement, but also a way of taking his scent and breath into her.

In the second position she puts her foot on his and begins to climb him while at the same time wrapping a leg and arm around him and pulling his shoulder down towards her. In addition to panting, she also begins to moan. Here the degree of blending is more advanced than in the first position because here, in addition to wrapping around the man she is also climbing him. Further, in the first "twining vine" position her panting is followed by resting and gazing at the man, whereas in the "climbing the tree" position her panting is followed by moaning. And even though the act of gazing can be seen as a form of visually penetrating and thus merging with the other person, in another way it also suggests the experience of distinctness from what is being gazed at. Moaning, on the other hand, seems to suggest the experience of a more complete merging. This is because moaning is typically done spontaneously without conscious thought. It thus indicates a loss of self-awareness and thus of the self–other distinction.

There is also the fact that in the first position the woman finds time to rest (which is why she is able to gaze), while in the second position, there is no resting; only panting and moaning. This points to the woman's rising excitement of taking the man into her. This further indicates a gradual loss of the experience of the distinction between herself and the man.

This progression continues into the next position. Here the woman and man are now lying down with thighs and arms entangled in a tight embrace. This points to yet a further degree of merging. In the earlier positions it was just one partner that was twining or wrapping around the other: now both are entangled. In addition, they are both here embracing tightly, something which can also be seen as pressing into and thus blending with each other. This loss of the sense of separation is underlined by the fact that in this position the participants are now lying down in an embrace. For to remain standing would suggest a sense of control that Vātsyāyana implies is now fading. We are further told that the embrace is so tight that they seem to be wrestling against one another. Now, although wrestling can be seen as an attempt to separate oneself from another person, it is also something in which each combatant is pressing into the other from many directions at once. That this is the sense that Vātsyāyana has in mind is evident not only from the metaphor of "rice-and-sesame" that is used to describe this position, but also from the description of the final position.

What is interesting about Vātsyāyana's description here is that the actual physical position seems to lose importance when compared with the experiential state of the participants. For here we are first given an account of their psychological states—"Blind with passion, oblivious to pain or injury"—and only subsequently told that "she may be on his lap, seated facing him, or on a bed." In addition, as the psychological states suggest, normal self-awareness seems well lost. Finally, and most significantly, Vātsyāyana says, "they embrace as if they would enter one another"; that is, the embrace displays the desire to (that is, "as if they would") enter into each other.

This remark is significant because it can be seen as the state that all of the positions he describes have been striving towards and thus purposely achieving in various forms and various degrees. Therefore, each of the sexual positions that Vātsyāyana gives can be seen as a rung in a ladder that leads to the participants' experience of entering into each other. Thus, the "twining vine" is the first step in moving towards another person in order to enter into and be entered into by that person. "Climbing the tree" approaches this goal to a further degree, as does "rice-and-sesame" in yet a deeper way. With the "milk-and-water" position the blending is complete.

Consequently, this experience of desirously entering into each other is something that each of these sexual positions shares in common to various degrees. Plainly, however, it is not just the four positions given by Vātsyāyana that share this feature; for there are numerous other positions that will also share it in varying degrees, including the man-on-top, woman-on-top, side-by-side, and rear-entry positions, plus all their variations. Vātsyāyana's positions are merely illustrative examples of the degrees which this feature can take. His examples are no doubt of sexual positions that were popular in India at the time.

Such positions are probably, to varying degrees, culturally determined. Carol Marks, for example, argues that in ancient Rome the woman-on-top position, in both its facing-towards and facing-away-from the man varieties, was the most common position,[8] whereas Kinsey and his co-workers marvelled at the nearly exclusive use of the man-on-top position that was the hallmark of heterosexual sexual life in America in the 1950s.[9] The man-on-top missionary position still seems to be the most common for long term-couples. But in one recent large survey, although the most preferred position by women was the man-on-top "missionary" position (30.9%), it was only slightly more preferred than the rear-entry "doggy" position (27.5%). The reverse was true for men.[10]

DESIROUSLY ENTERING INTO EACH OTHER

Despite possible cultural reasons for the adoption of certain positions, if done for sexual reasons, they all nevertheless share the feature of the participants' experience of desiring to enter into each other. And it is precisely this experience that gives the erotic and sexually exciting features, and thus the erotic meaning, to the sexual positions. This is why the woman in Vātsyāyana's examples becomes more and more sexually excited with each progressive position: from gazing, to panting, to moaning, to both partners being blind with passion. For with each position she finds herself entering her partner more and more while simularly being entered into by her partner. This erotic meaning of "entering into each other" is what remains once the interpersonal-orientation meanings have been disengaged.

What distinguishes the positions in terms of erotic meaning, then, is the degree to and manner in which this experience of entering into each other is achieved. To see how this works, however, it is important not to equate the idea of "entering" with the idea of the penis penetrating the vagina. This is frequently an important feature of the experience of entering and being entered and people, both men and women, often prefer a position because of the depth of penile penetration they feel it allows. Thus, one man describing what he likes about the rear-entry position says, "It feels like I'm going deeper."[11] Similarly, a woman states, "I really like doggy-style . . . I enjoy deep penetration, and this position sure does that."[12]

But it is not the sole aspect of the idea here of entering in a sexual position. This is because the idea of entering into each other carries with it the idea that not only is the man entering into the woman, but the woman is also entering into the man. This is possible because the penis' penetration of the vagina is only one form of the experience of entering into or being entered by another body. One can also have the experience of entering into or being entered into in oral sex, deep kissing, biting, finger sucking, and in numerous other sexual practices. Indeed, the simple mutual caressing of a naked body by another naked body can give rise to the sensation of each person entering into the other. Because of this it can be that sexual intercourse is also experienced by the participants as the woman entering into the man.[13]

Thus, one woman says that what she particularly likes about the man-on-top "missionary" position is that "You've got constant skin-on-skin contact and can feel every inch of each other with your hands."[14] She does not elaborate on this point. But it is in just such mutual caressing through constant skin-to-skin contact that a sense of entering into and being entered by one's partner can easily occur. It seems likely, therefore, that at least one of the things she enjoys about this sort of contact is the sense of entering and being entered into that it gives rise to. She also refers to the partners being able to feel every inch of each other with their hands in this position. Here too we have a mutual caressing of naked bodies, which in turn can similarly lead to a sense of interpenetration of bodies. Both of her comments—constant skin-on-skin contact and hands over every part of each other's bodies—refer also to the manner in which the entering into each other is experienced. For as she describes this position there is no particular point of contact through which the mutual entering seems to take place. Rather, the position as she experiences it is a global one in which the constant and numerous points of contact would seem to facilitate a diffuse and overall sense of merging.

Therefore, what is crucial here is not the actual physical entering, but the experience of such an entering, what might be called the experiential entering. This is something that may or may not take place in the physical joining of bodies. This is why even a physical quality like the depth of penile penetration, which was mentioned above, does not in itself necessarily carry an erotic meaning. Penile penetration can be engaged in for numerous non-sexual reasons, as, for example, when the desire behind the penetration is primarily to express an interpersonal-orientation meaning. The psychoanalyst Wilhelm Reich, for example, refers to men who see penetration as a form of aggression and see their penises as a stabbing instrument to be used against the woman.[15] Therefore, such penetration only carries an erotic meaning for the participant if he or she experiences it as desirously entering another body or being thus entered into by another body.

Here we also see how the meaning of "desirously entering into each other" serves to distinguish the erotic meanings of the different positions. For in the different positions a person can experience himself or herself as entering or being entered into in various degrees and in various ways by the other person. In each case, sofar as it is experienced as an entering into, it will be perceived as two bodies that merge into and partake of each other by crossing over each other's boundaries. However, the manner in and degree to which the crossing over takes place will alter fundamentally according to how one organizes it in awareness. In this way the sexual position as an element in the participants' awareness is best understood as an interpenetrating two-body Gestalt. This is because the configuration of a particular sexual position is more than the sum of its parts: at any one moment it can be viewed in numerous distinct ways.

To take an example, let us consider the woman-on-top position. In this position, with the woman sitting and facing the man, the woman can perceive herself as being entered from below as she envelopes the man's erection with her vagina. Here she also straddles the man and, if she engages in pelvic thrusting, may have a sense of sucking the man's pelvic region up into herself. Because of the minimal bodily contact in this position—with contact being typically limited to the genitals, lower pelvic region and the inside of the thighs—the woman might be able more easily to focus her awareness on the genital enveloping that is taking place. In this case she could well experience the position as offering a moment of being deeply entered into, underlined with a sense of gradually drawing the man's body up into hers. Because, however, of the limited body contact, the manner of her being entered into could easily be sensed as being sharply focused on the point of physical entry, namely, her vagina. This stands in clear contrast to the woman just mentioned and her preference for the man-on-top position. In that case the experience of the manner of desirously entering into each other seems to have no particular point of focus. It is simply spread out over the entire body.

However, in the example of the woman-on-top position, despite the deepness of the penetration, the man's face in this position nevertheless exists at a distance from the woman's face. For another woman, or the same woman at another time, this distance over which she must gaze in order to have eye contact with the man might easily serve to create an element of distance in the experience of bodily penetration. (This might be one of the reasons why some women who prefer the woman-on-top position prefer it when they are facing away from the man.) Also kissing or embracing, which seem typically expressions of intimacy and which are often involved in sexual intercourse, are not possible in this position. To kiss or embrace her partner the woman must—partially, at least—abandon this position and lean forward to have her face and upper body come in contact with the man's. This, along with the fact that she has to maintain enough control to remain sitting upright (if she is to continue in this position) might serve to lessen the sense of deepness and completeness of the experience of being entered.

Further, even though the minimal bodily contact in this position might allow some women to focus more easily on the erotic meaning of absorbing her partner into her, other aspects of this position might work against this awareness. As one woman says, "I know girl-on-top is supposed to be ah-mazing . . . . But, as much as I hate to admit it, I'm too insecure to really enjoy myself that way. I'm thinking, am I going at the right pace? Do I look funny when I lean down? Are those my knees popping? I like missionary because it makes me feel more secure and lets me concentrate on how everything feels."[16] Although it is unclear, it is possible that the phrase "how everything feels" refers to the same sort of more global experience mention by the woman referred to earlier who also preferred the missionary position.

With this it should be clear that there is no erotic meaning that could be said to be intrinsic to a sexual position. For the erotic meaning of each position will depend on how the participants at each moment interpret the experience. Further, it will not even be true that the experience of the highest degree of entering into or being entered by one's partner will be the goal of each person's enactment of a sexual position. For it may well be that what is desired in a particular instance by a particular person is only a minimal degree of entering or being entered. Nevertheless, sofar as the sexual position chosen carries an erotic meaning, that meaning will have do to with the experience of entering into each other.

3
Sex Hormones and Sexual Desire

THE BIOLOGICAL VIEW OF SEXUAL DESIRE

Having established that sexual desire lies at the basis of why gender is of such importance to us, it is natural to raise the question of why human beings have sexual desire. This is a question that has been answered in various ways by different scholars. Those taking a biological approach to human sexuality typically argue for a biological basis for sexual desire. They point to findings that are meant to show that sexual desire has its origins in specific biological processes and, consequently, that without these processes there would be no sexual desire. In other words, certain biological processes are necessary, though not sufficient, for the existence of sexual desire. In this essay I shall argue that such a biologically based view of human sexual desire is ill-founded and not supported by the data. This does not mean, however, that the biological processes in question have no relation to sexual desire, but only that their role is inessential and, consequently, that human sexual desire is not dependent in any fundamental sense on such biological processes. I will then offer a phenomenological or experiential account of the contingent relation these processes have to sexual desire.

Before I approach this topic, however, it will be helpful to get clear about what is meant by the term "sexual desire." This is because there are several phenomena that are related to but nevertheless distinct from sexual desire and which, as a result, can be easily confused with sexual desire. These phenomena include sexual arousal and other physiological sexual processes like vaginal lubrication, erection of the penis, or the rapid muscular contractions of orgasm. If processes like these are not clearly distinguished from sexual desire, or mistakenly thought to be the essence of sexual desire, difficulties will appear. One can, for example, run the risk of thinking that because a biological process is essential for, say, sexual arousal or a physiological sexual event, it must consequently be essential for sexual desire.

But what are the reasons for drawing a distinction between sexual desire and these other sexual phenomena? The answer is that any of these phenomena can occur in the absence of sexual desire. Thus, genital stimulation, for example, can lead to the physiological events of sexual arousal, vaginal lubrication, erection, or even orgasm, without the person experiencing sexual desire.[1] This fact is the basis of Helen Singer Kaplan's model of the sexual process that explains sexual desire as an independent element in the process.[2] Further, although sexual desire can also lead to physiological sexual responses, sexual desire frequently takes place without these accompanying responses.[3] Consequently, sexual desire is distinct from such biological events.

What, then, is sexual desire? One answer is that sexual desire is an experience and thus must be understood in terms of the structure of awareness. I elsewhere propose such a view, arguing that sexual desire is the experience of desire for the *mutual* baring and caressing of bodies (as physical expressions of mutual vulnerability and care), which may or may not involve the genitals, and which may involve a real, symbolic, or fantasized other person. Here the gender of the other person's body—be it the same or a different gender—is seen phenomenologically to complete the sense of gender that one has of one's own body, that is, to fill an experiential void or emptiness that lies at the heart of the experience of gender. In heterosexual desire it is the opposite gender that is felt to give a sense of completion to this emptiness, while in homosexual desire it is the same gender that is felt to do this. For bisexual desire it can be either. This is a view that I shall present more fully in the next essay.

This answer, however, still leaves open the question of why human beings experience such a desire. This is because proponents of competing explanations of the origin of sexual desire, such as social constructionism, the biological view, and the phenomenological view could easily agree that sexual desire is an experience, but then go on to disagree about how this experience has its genesis. Social constructionists might argue that the experience of sexual desire is something that culture has somehow constructed and placed within us. The phenomenological view, however, is that sexual desire is an existential need that has its origins in the experience of the incompleteness of gender. I shall consider both of these views in the next essay, rejecting social constructionism and arguing for the phenomenological. For now I turn to the biological view.

Scholars with a biological view of human sexuality often draw a distinction between what has been called ultimate and proximate causes.[4] Ultimate causes refer to the evolutionary history of a behaviour or experience, which can be seen as the "ultimate cause" of a present behaviour or experience. On the other hand, proximate causes refer to the evolutionary biological structures or processes that biologically-orientated scholars believe assume an essential role in the immediate causes of a present behaviour or experience.

Although scholars giving a biological account of the nature of sexual desire are keen to explain the ultimate or evolutionary history of sexual desire,[5] it is plain that for any biological theory to be viable one must also be able to give an account of the proximate causes of sexual desire. That is, one must be able to point to the biological structures or processes that play a necessary role in the cause of the experience of sexual desire. This does not mean scholars who attempt to do this discount the role of non-biological elements in sexual desire, or that biological elements are sufficient for sexual desire, but only that they see certain biological factors as having a decisive role in the experience of sexual desire.

But what are the biological factors that are thought to play such a part in sexual desire? The most common answer given is sex hormones, that is, the biochemical secretions that are primarily responsible for the development and maintenance of the biological sex characteristics—both the sex organs and internal reproductive systems, and the secondary sex characteristics. These classes of hormones, namely progesterone, oestrogen, and androgen, are produced mainly by the testes in the male or the ovaries in the female. Sex hormones are clearly related to biological aspects of human sexuality, and even to sexual behaviour in non-human animals. This has made several biologically-orientated researchers feel that the actions of sex hormones might also explain the existence of human sexual desire. This does not imply, however, that environmental stimuli are not seen to play a part in the appearance of sexual desire,[6] but only that the presence of sex hormones are necessary for sexual desire to take place. This is a position that is widely held.[7]

One view of how this works is that sex hormones act directly on the central nervous system to cause and maintain sexual desire.[8] Another is they act on genital sensory receptors or afferent pathways to the central nervous system to lower the threshold for genital sensation. This leads to the activation of these receptors, which then directly gives rise to sexual desire.[9]

Although it is androgen in particular that is thought to play a role, even in females,[10] some researchers suggest that, in the female, progesterone and oestrogen might also be circuitously involved. It might be that, in some situations, progesterone and oestrogen allow androgen to have an effect by them subsiding to low levels of concentration.[11] Again, it is generally allowed that the higher order functions of the brain can heavily moderate the action of sex hormones.[12] In other words, although sex hormones are necessary for sexual desire, they are not sufficient. Because of this, non-biological factors can easily influence or override a hormone's effect—such as when a person motivated by sexual desire to approach another person, perceives the desired person to be rejecting his or her advances, which is why sex hormones are not sufficient for the existence of sexual desire.

This is why some researchers prefer to say that hormones do not cause behaviour, but rather alter the probabilities that a behaviour will take place in a certain situation.[13] This, however, does not go against the view that such hormones are still a necessary component for the experience of sexual desire. Many researchers allow that the presence of sex hormones is not sufficient for sexual desire, while still maintaining that their presence is necessary. Ganz and Greendale, for example, claim that "a large body of evolving information about sexual functioning (and dysfunction) suggests that these hormones [i.e., ovarian sex hormones] may be necessary but not sufficient to overcome disorders of desire [i.e., loss of desire] and arousal in women."[14] This view is succinctly stated by Rako who, discussing women and sexual desire, says, "sexual desire is influenced by many factors—relational, situational, psychological, and physical", and yet, "whatever other factors may be playing in a woman's loss of interest in making love, without adequate testosterone [an androgen], sexual desire simply cannot exist."[15]

SEX HORMONES AND MALE SEXUAL DESIRE

What, then, is the evidence for this view? Let us start by having a look at the relation between sex hormones and sexual desire in the male. While arguing for the necessary role that hormones play in sexual desire, John Bancroft says, "an adult male's continued interest in sex depends on his having a normal level of circulating testosterone. If an otherwise normal male has his testosterone lowered by testicular suppressive drugs, he experiences a decline in sexual interest, which returns when the process is reversed."[16] The same thing occurs when testosterone levels decline due to testicular impairment. In this situation, we are told, males experience a lowering of both sexual interest and the ability to ejaculate. Further, spontaneous nocturnal erections come and go according to whether testosterone is withdrawn or replaced.[17] All of this, it is claimed, clearly shows that testosterone is necessary for normal levels of sexual desire, a term that he uses interchangeably with the term "sexual interest".

But do these findings really support this conclusion? Several points count against such a claim. First, it should be seen that the findings concerning the decline of nocturnal erections tell us nothing about the effects of testosterone withdrawal on sexual desire. They only tell us about the effects of testosterone withdrawal on nocturnal erections. Nothing indicates that sexual desire has been affected by the withdrawal of testosterone, especially since there is no obvious connection between a man's ability to have sexual desire and his ability to have nocturnal erections. The physiology of nocturnal erections is poorly understood and nocturnal erections, which seem to have a relation to REM sleep might well be a physiological reaction that has little to do with sexual desire.[18] Further, even if nocturnal erections were caused by, say, sexual desire experienced while dreaming, this does not mean that the disappearance of nocturnal erections indicates the disappearance of sexual desire while dreaming. The question remains an open one and more research is needed. Still, it seems just as plausible that the withdrawal of testosterone has merely hindered the ability to have erections, not the ability to have sexual desire.

In different cases of erectile failure it can well be that the man has sexual desire but that other factors, like anxiety or biological problems, interfere with his ability to have or maintain an erection.[19] If erectile failure in such cases need not indicate a loss of sexual desire, it seems the same would hold in this case. That is, a decrease in nocturnal erections need not imply the man has a decrease in sexual desire.

Secondly, the same research that Bancroft cites to support his claim about the reduction of sexual desire as a response to testicular suppressive drugs also shows that, in addition to being related to a decline in sexual desire, such drugs are further related to a "marked decrease in the frequency of spontaneous erections" along with "a strong trend towards decreased ability to maintain an erection during intercourse."[20] But if this is true, might it not be the decreased ability to have erections—along with the meaning assigned by the man to this decreased ability—that is essentially responsible for the decline in sexual desire? This is also a plausible account. In this view, testosterone levels are only incidentally involved (so far as they lead to a decreased ability to have erections). The crucial factor is the meaning this decreased ability has for the man.

This interpretation is suggested by the fact that the reduced ability to have or maintain an erection or to ejaculate, especially during sexual intercourse, is a powerful social stigma. A man with this sort of erectile or ejaculatory dysfunction is typically seen to be unmasculine or unvirile. It causes a man considerable distress, loss of self-esteem, and adversely affects his relationships, which is probably one of the reasons why the drug sildenafil, with its ability to help cause and maintain erections, has been so popular.[21] It seems likely, therefore, that many males afflicted in this way would be uncomfortable in a sexual situation and so prefer to avoid sexual interactions, especially if their partners also showed discomfort or displeasure under such circumstances.

Someone in this situation who was aware of his erectile or ejaculatory problems and was thus avoiding sexual encounters could easily begin to feel he has lost his sexual desire. This much follows from Festinger's theory of cognitive dissonance.[22] Most males, it seems, would find it a dissonant situation to experience sexual desire while at the same time having erection problems and avoiding sexual interaction. If one has sexual desire—the reasoning might go—then it seems one should neither have trouble having erections nor avoid sexual encounters. One way to dissipate the cognitive dissonance generated would be to attempt to suppress or deny one's sexual desire, or at least the awareness of one's sexual desire.

Further, it appears likely that a man in this situation would also prefer to avoid activities that might lead to sexual intercourse, or at least those activities that might be taken by the woman to imply that the man is interested in sexual intercourse. This would explain Bagetell et al.'s findings that there was also a decline in kissing and fondling subsequent to the withdrawal of testosterone.[23] This is because if a man engages in the kissing and fondling of a woman, the woman could, depending on the circumstances, easily interpret this as a display of the man's desire to proceed to sexual intercourse. But if the woman were then to act on the man's seeming advances and invite him to have sexual intercourse with her, the man would be left in the humiliating position of not being able to follow through on an offer that he seemed to be courting, an offer that she would probably expect him to accept. This is because an erection is necessary for effective sexual intercourse.

In such a state of affairs it might seem wiser for the man to avoid kissing and fondling or any other behaviour that might be taken as an indication of his desire for sexual intercourse. In this interpretation, then, the lowering of sexual desire is a combined result of the lowered ability to have erections and ejaculations, a perception of the social stigma attached to such reduced abilities, and a desire to avoid this stigma. Here, the withdrawal of sex hormones, which causes the decrease in erections and capacity for ejaculation, plays no essential role in the lowering of sexual desire. This is because it is not essential that the man perceives or responds to the social stigma in this way. If he were unconcerned about the social stigma, or had a partner that was unconcerned, then despite the lowering of sex hormone levels, he might well persist in having sexual desire. He may have difficulty engaging in sexual intercourse, but that is another matter.

This conclusion is strongly supported by what is known about the sexual desires and sexual activities of eunuchs. Eunuchs are males who have been castrated (that is, had their testicles removed) and thus suffer a state of permanent testosterone deficiency. The practice of castration was carried out in numerous cultures; from Rome, Byzantium, to different Islamic societies and ancient China. In many of these cultures eunuchs were employed as harem attendants or guards. The castration was done to keep the attendants or guards from sexually interacting with the women or getting the women pregnant.

However, although the state of castration may have stopped eunuchs from impregnating their women charges, it did not stop them from having sexual desire towards the women or from having sexual intercourse with them. As

Michael Aucoin and Richard Wassersug have shown, there is much evidence that such harem eunuchs continued to have sexual desire and were sexually active with the women.[24] The mediaeval Islamic writer Bayhaî, for example, tells us that "the eunuchs have a strong lust for and an amazing attraction to women."[25] Thus, says Ayalon, in mediaeval Islamic culture "sexual relations of various forms with eunuchs were very common, as it seems, everywhere. The eunuchs did not lose their sexual desire, either as active or passive partners."[26]

Some contemporary scholars have disputed these claims, but the evidence clearly suggests that eunuchs did have sexual desire. Ringrose, for example, says of eunuchs "most, but not all, of them lost all interest in sexual activity."[27] Unfortunately, she cites no sources to back up her claim, a claim which goes against numerous mediaeval sources.[28] Further, Ringrose herself points out that Chinese and Islamic cultures "frowned upon expressions of sexual pleasure of any kind between women of the court and their servants, making total ablation [removal of not just the testicles but also the penis] necessary."[29] This shows that simple removal of the testicles was not enough to quash "expressions of sexual pleasure" and stop the eunuch from having sexual intercourse with his female charges. And of course the removal of the penis did not get rid of sexual desire; it only got rid of the possibility of expressing that desire through sexual intercourse. As Aucoin and Wassersug say, the totally ablated eunuch still had his hands and mouth through which he could express his sexual desires.

One could always protest that the sexual desire that eunuchs feel may not be the same sort of sexual desire that the intact testosterone-sufficient male feels. There is, however, no evidence to support such a view, a view that seems little more than a last minute attempt to deny the evidence that eunuchs can have "real" sexual desire.

Also, not only did eunuchs maintain their sexual desire, but they were even sexually desired by women. The writings of Gahiz, for example, present eunuchs as being sexually desired by women because they were slow to ejaculate and carried no risk of impregnating their partners.[30] Similarly, Bayhaqî says, "one of the merits of the eunuch is that the woman is attracted to him because he is safer and she covets him because he is forbidden to her and because she is secure from having a child [from him]"[31] This shows that far from being stigmatized, a eunuch might even be sexually desired.

But why then is it that testosterone-deprived males in these pre-modern cultures continued to have sexual desire, whereas various modern studies purport to show that androgen deprived males have no sexual desire?[32] The answer, as I have suggested, has do with social rather than biological factors. If a man is sexually desired because of his testosterone-deprived state, as many eunuchs in earlier times were, then being slow to ejaculate, or slow to have an erection, which is part of the testosterone-deprived state, need not be seen by the man as a stigma. Consequently, there is no need for him to try to suppress his sexual desire or avoid sexual activities. What all of this suggests is that a male's sexual desire is not dependent on sex hormone levels in any fundamental way.

SEX HORMONES AND FEMALE SEXUAL DESIRE

Concerning females, several scholars have also argued for the essential role of sex hormones in sexual behaviour and desire. Thus Bartlik and Kaplan claim that "for a woman to live with inadequate levels of testosterone is no small matter. For many it means the complete inability to experience sexual desire, sexual fantasy, arousal and/or orgasm." "Female sexuality without testosterone," they say "is a house without a foundation."[33] Yet an examination of the evidence shows that with females the relevance of sex hormones in sexual behaviour and experience is even more unclear than it is with males. When the situations that involve a fluctuation in a woman's sex hormones are studied in order to observe for any changes in sexual desire, the results are typically inconsistent.

Thus, although some women seem to have increased sexual desire when they are ovulating or reduced sexual desire when they are menstruating, many more notice no such change in their sexual desire or experience different changes.[34] In addition, although some women seem to lose sexual desire when taking oral contraceptives (drugs that decrease testosterone levels),[35] other women plainly experience no change in their sexual desire or even have heightened sexual desire. Likewise, breast-feeding, which is also related to changing levels of sex hormones, has no consistent effect on a woman's levels of sexual desire. As we shall see, while some women who breast-feed appear to display a decline in sexual desire, others do not. A similar picture holds for women undergoing menopause, another situation in which women display a variation in levels of sex hormones. Again, some women seem to feel a decline in sexual desire while others do not.[36]

Further, in each of these cases where there is a change in sexual desire, several non-hormonal explanations are readily available. This is not to say that the non-hormonal explanations must be the correct ones—further research is needed to establish that—but only that their plausibility means we are not compelled to accept the hormonal explanation. The rise in sexual desire that some women experience during ovulation might be explained by certain events associated with ovulation that help to focus a woman's awareness on her pelvic and genital region during ovulation. Many women experience lower abdominal discomfort or sensations during the time of ovulation or, again, many women notice a vaginal discharge (cervical mucous) during ovulation.[37] These events direct the woman's attention to her genitals and so could be precursors to a rise in sexual desire. As I have argued in *The Nature of Sexual Desire*, genital stimulation—and, with women, deeper stimulations of the uterus and related organs—whether from internal or external sources, can readily lead to the beginnings of sexual arousal, which in turn can give rise to sexual desire. I shall explore this view later in this essay when I present a phenomenological account of the working of sex hormones.

Similarly, the decline in sexual desire that some women experience when menstruating is quite explicable in terms of feelings of disgust that some people associate with menstruation and having sexual contact during menstruation.[38] All of this agrees with Hedricks' review of the literature concerning female sexual activity across the menstrual cycle.[39] Here she concludes that it is social rather than endocrine factors that are most likely to contribute to the variance of psychological states across the female menstrual cycle. In the case of the effects of oral contraceptives on sexual behaviour there are also several non-hormonal explanations available. For the woman who seems to lose sexual desire it might simply be that the presence of an abnormal endocrinological situation makes her feel unwell, a situation that puts her off desiring sexual activity. Or again, a woman might be ambivalent about taking oral contraceptives. Even though she does not want to get pregnant and thus takes her contraceptives, perhaps she also has religious or moral feelings that go against the use of contraceptives. Or perhaps she is strongly aware of the health risks involved in the use of oral contraceptives. In such situations it is understandable that the resulting feelings of guilt, disappointment, or concern might work to mitigate her feelings of desire.

On the other hand, a woman might not respond negatively to the altered endocrinology caused by oral contraceptives. She might also see the use of oral contraceptives as being a path to freedom from the fear of unwanted pregnancy. Perhaps she also sees the health risks, but sees them as being minor compared to all the risks involved in an unwanted pregnancy. In this situation the woman might well experience no change in her sexual desire or even a release from anxieties surrounding sexual intercourse and so experience a heightening of sexual desire.

Here we have explanations for the various responses to oral contraceptives that have nothing to do with hormonal fluctuations but instead have to do with the attachment of meaning to the act of taking oral contraceptives.

In the same way, it is understandable that, for some women, the physiological activity involved in breast-feeding, the associated sore breasts, being kept awake for night breast-feeding—not to mention all the other tasks of motherhood—might, through exhaustion, take its toll on the desire to engage in sexual activity. Rowland et al., for example, found that out of 181 new mothers who were currently breast-feeding, 167 had not yet resumed sexual intercourse. When asked why, the answer "being too tired" (given by 16.8%) was the second most common, preceded only by "lack of interest" (given by

18.6%) (215 different reasons were given, with 54 subjects giving more than one reason.) And even the answer "lack of interest" might well be simply an expression of being too tired; for it is very understandable that one lacks interest when one is too tired. The other most common answers were "being afraid of intercourse being painful" (16.8%), "physician told them not to" (15.6%), and "thinking they should wait 6 weeks" (14.4%), not that they had no sexual desire.[40]

Further, it is important to note that Hyde et al.'s study[41] on sexuality during pregnancy and the postpartum year does not, as Bancroft[42] claims, support the view that there tends to be decline in sexual interest in women who breast-feed. Although this research found that women who were breast-feeding were less likely to engage in sexual intercourse than those who were not breastfeeding, there was no difference between the two groups for their likelihood to engage in masturbation, fellatio, or cunnilingus. This strongly suggests that sexual desire remains fully intact during breast-feeding; for masturbation, fellatio, or cunnilingus are also usually expressions of sexual desire. Consequently, what is affected is simply the incidence of sexual intercourse.

And this is understandable: for breast-feeding is associated with the suppression of oestrogen, a hormone that functions to maintain the vaginal lining and lubrication.[43] As a result, sexual intercourse will tend to be more uncomfortable for breast-feeding women than for those who do not breastfeed, and breast-feeding women may thus tend to avoid sexual intercourse. This is suggested in Rowland et al.'s study where in the third most common reason for breast-feeding women avoiding sexual intercourse is "being afraid of intercourse being painful."[44] But avoiding sexual intercourse for this reason has nothing to do with a decline in sexual desire.

Similar difficulties can be found with the view that, during menopause a decline in sex hormones leads to a decline in sexual desire. One problem is that there is evidence to suggest that apparent declines in sexual desire at this time in a woman's life are more related to age than to menopausal status.[45] Though here, it should be noted, it is likely that any such decline has more to do more with the increase in health problems often associated with aging—and with the medications used to treat such problems—than with aging itself.[46]

Moreover, even in those instances of declining sexual desire that do appear to be a response to menopause, nothing forces us to see this as being dependent on the fluctuation of hormones. Since many women see menstruation and fertility as a fundamental aspect of their femininity,[47] it is clear that many women, and men too, interpret menopause as a loss of a woman's femininity, youth, and sexual desirability, rather than as, say, freedom from having to use menstrual products or freedom from the fear of unwanted pregnancy.

With such meanings looming in a woman's and her sexual partner's awareness, a woman might well experience a decline of sexual desire. For again, if a woman sees her own sexual desire as being connected to her femininity, youth, and sexual desirability, as many women clearly do, then it is a cognitively dissonant situation to think one has maintained the former while losing the latter. One way to reduce the dissonance here would be for the woman to try to convince herself that she no longer has sexual desire.

A couple of often-cited studies that seem to go against this view of menopause are those by Barbara Sherwin and her co-workers, researchers who examined the effects of surgically induced menopause and hormone replacement. In one double-blind study Sherwin et al. randomly assigned surgically menopausal women (women whose menopause was artificially induced by hysterectomy) into one of three hormone replacement groups: one group receiving oestrogen and androgen, one receiving androgen alone, one receiving oestrogen alone, and one receiving a placebo. They also had a control group, namely women with hysterectomies who received neither replacement hormones nor placebo. They then measured each groups' sexual functioning, which they defined as level of sexual desire, number of sexual fantasies, level of arousal during intercourse, frequency of intercourse, and frequency of orgasm. The results, they claimed, showed that exogenous androgen increased the intensity of sexual desire and arousal, and the frequency of sexual fantasies, but not sexual intercourse or orgasm.[48]

This study, however, is flawed in several ways. First, all the subjects were women who had recently undergone traumatic sexual surgery. This is a problem because, as de Marquiegui and Huish argue, disfiguring operations on a woman's reproductive organs (or face, breasts, or genitals), frequently have a damaging effect on her sexuality.[49] This makes the subjects into an unrepresentative group.

Secondly, subjects in the control group were both significantly younger than the rest of the subjects and also all had their ovaries intact (Several of the subjects in the other groups had their ovaries removed.) This introduces a significant difference between the control and treatment subjects. These factors severely confound the results rendering their interpretation and generalizability problematic.

Thirdly, various results were found that went contrary to the hypotheses. Thus, although the testosterone levels of each the treatment groups were expected to fall during a one month placebo phase of the study, for some inexplicable reason the testosterone levels for the oestrogen–androgen group did not fall.

Fourthly, although the authors claim that the "androgenic effects on sexual desire, arousal, and fantasy" increased with the time since surgery, this also happened for the control group, which received no replacement androgen. This suggests that time since surgery was also a confounding variable. These findings make it difficult to draw any clear interpretation of the study.

In another study Sherwin and Gelfand took women who had also undergone hysterectomies, including the removal of both ovaries, and divided them into groups that received no treatment, oestrogen replacement, or oestrogen–testosterone replacement. Of these, only the oestrogen–testosterone group showed an increase in sexual desire, as they also did in sexual fantasies, arousal, intercourse, and orgasms. These results were again interpreted as showing that testosterone increases, among other things, sexual desire.[50]

Here too, however, there are various problems. Again, the subjects were women who have been traumatized through sexual surgery. Also, not only were the subjects not randomly assigned into their groups but, further, the study does not seem to be double blind. That is, it appears that the researchers knew which group was receiving testosterone and, also, that the subjects in each group knew if they were receiving testosterone.

This creates an experimental bias because testosterone has a mystique as a "powerful sex hormone" and even as an aphrodisiac. Germaine Greer, for example, in her popular book *The Change: Women, Aging, and Menopause*, warns about the administration of testosterone to perimenopausal women since it "will bring about an instant increase in genital sensitivity" that, with single women, "can only lead into dangerous and compromising situations or humiliating bouts of masturbation."[51] She also sees the administration of testosterone to women as an attempt to tailor women's sexuality to men's and refers to testosterone as a "male hormone," a view that seems to be held by many women: findings indicate that 95% of women in North America do not know that a woman's body normally produces testosterone.[52] These finding were, however, from 1999. Still, my impression is that popular knowledge on this has not changed drastically since then.

It is very possible, therefore, that an expectancy for increased sexual functioning could easily have affected both the researchers' treatment of the subjects and the subjects' responses (Compare, for example, Wilson and Lawson's study where male subjects showed increased sexual arousal to viewing erotic films simply because they believed [falsely] they had ingested alcohol—another drug that is popularly, though mistakenly, believed to be a stimulant of sexual desire.)[53]

Most importantly, although in both these studies Sherwin and her coworkers imply that testosterone was the immediate common cause for the increase in all the variables studied, nothing in their results requires this interpretation. For the design of their study does not enable them to rule out other possible causal relations. It is quite possible that although the testosterone might have caused an increase in physiological arousal, it was an awareness of and meaning attached to the heightened arousal that led to the increase in sexual desire and the other behaviours. Again, an awareness of the bodily and especially genital changes during the sexual process might well lead to an increase in sexual desire. It is important to remember that, as mentioned earlier, sexual physiological arousal and sexual desire are distinct phenomena and that the former can easily occur without the later.

Finally, even if the administered testosterone were somehow causally responsible for the subjects' increased sexual desire, this does not show that naturally occurring testosterone levels have any relation to sexual desire in women. In a large study of over 1,000 randomly selected women between 18 and 75 years old, Davis et al. found that naturally occurring testosterone levels had no correlation with a woman's sexual desire, arousal, pleasure, orgasmic ability, or sexual self-image.[54]

This gives even more credibility to the non-hormonal explanations that are readily available to account for such cases of fluctuation in female sexual desire, fluctuations that, it must be remembered, occur in only a portion of women. Such considerations raise a large question mark over what research has shown us about female sexual desire having its origins in the ebb and flow of sex hormones.

Moreover, the fact that females show a less clear relation between levels of sex hormones and levels of sexual desire is just what one would expect if my interpretation of the male response to fluctuating sex hormone levels is correct. There I suggested that a lowering of male sexual desire might well be a result of both the inability to have or maintain erections or to ejaculate and concerns about the social stigmas attached to such inabilities. If this is what is happening in the male situation, then it seems likely that a similar account, with due alteration of details, could be applied to the female situation. Here too, what sex hormones are necessary for are sexual physiological responses, not sexual desire.

Yet, in the female, there are no obvious physiological events upon which she depends in order to engage adequately in sexual intercourse. That is, although a male's ability to have what is seen as successful sexual intercourse is dependent on his ability to have erections and to ejaculate, there are no similar physiological requirements upon which the female's ability depends. Even though the physiological events of vaginal engorgement and lubrication can facilitate a woman's ability to have and enjoy intercourse, they are far from necessary: the vagina can be penetrated whether or not it is engorged and the vagina is often sufficiently lubricated without sexually induced lubrication, or saliva or an artificial lubricant can be used. And, what is more significant, the non-occurrence of such vaginal changes is not obvious to her sexual partner in the way that his lack of erection or ejaculation is obvious to her.[55]

In addition, and even more importantly, there is little social stigma attached to a female who fails to display such physiological events, especially when we compare it to the stigma attached to the male who lacks the ability to become erect or ejaculate. And this lack of stigma is quite explicable, for not only will the male find it difficult to know if these events have taken place in the female (and thus find it difficult to know when to stigmatize her) but, further, her ability to satisfy him in sexual intercourse does not depend on these events. This would give him little reason to stigmatize her. It is true that there is some stigma attached to the non-orgasmic or "frigid" woman, but again, whether or not a woman has had an orgasm is something her partner cannot typically know, especially if she does not want him to know—which is probably at least one of the reasons why women report pretending to have orgasms much more than men do.[56]

This means, then, that there are no obvious hormone-dependent events that take place in female sexual activity or biology that females can expect to be stigmatized for not having. Consequently, a woman with reduced levels of sex hormones need not avoid sexual interactions for fear of being humiliated or stigmatized. This further means that there is no reason for her, as there is for the male, to show a reduction of sexual desire as a result of the awareness that her physiological situation prevents her from engaging in sexual intercourse and satisfying her partner.

Such an account makes it fairly clear why females show more variation in a hormone-related lowering of sexual desire than males do; for being largely free from concerns about social stigmas over their sexual physiological functioning, womens' individual differences are given more scope for expression. As with the male, one is able to give an account that does not require the assumption that sex hormones are necessary for the existence of sexual desire.

SEX HORMONES AND ANIMALS

At this point someone will probably want to object that findings from animal studies paint a different picture of the role of sex hormones. With non-human mammals, it might be claimed; the crucial role of sex hormones in giving rise to both sexual behaviour and sexual desire has been well established. Consequently, it could be argued, even though there may be variation in the apparent effects of sex hormones on different people, and even though there may be other non-hormonal explanations for such effects, the fact that sex hormones play a necessary role in the sexual behaviour and desire of non-human mammals makes it likely that they also play such a role in human sexual desire.

The problem, however, is that the category "mammalian species" is a vast one, with some species being phylogenically close to us, and others being phylogenically remote from us. Plainly, it is those species phylogenically closest to us whose behaviour is the most relevant here. These species are the non-human anthropoid primates, namely the apes and monkeys. Significantly, it is just with these species that sexual behaviour and desire seems least dependent on sex hormones.

For example, several studies of castrated non-human anthropoid males, in both confined and free-ranging populations, show that these animals are unique among non-human mammals in being able to continue to show not only sexual interest, but also sexual activity after castration.[57] It is true that sexual interest and activity in these cases tend to be reduced, but not always. Loy, for example, observed a free-ranging male rhesus monkey who, seven years after being castrated, was still mounting and penetrating females, and even showing the characteristic ejaculatory pause associated with the intact male's ejaculation.[58] This anthropoid ability to continue to show sexual interest after castration contrasts starkly with the primate group that is phylogenically furthest removed from human beings, namely the prosimians (lemurs, lorisines, and tarsiers). Here castration seems to kill male sexual desire and activity.[59]

Likewise, it is clear that with non-human anthropoid females, sexual receptivity (female acceptance of male initiation of sexual behaviour) and proceptivity (female initiation of sexual behaviour), are far less tied to the ovarian cycle than is the case with prosimian females, whose ovarian cycles, unlike the anthropoids, show no menstruation. The bonobo or pigmy chimpanzee, for example, is the most sexually active of the non-human primates, with sexual behaviour being shown frequently in numerous situations. Although the female tends to be more attractive to the male when she exhibits her monthly hormone-induced genital swelling, a female will show both receptivity and proceptivity at any time during her menstrual cycle.[60] For example, female bonobos frequently will offer sexual intercourse to males (and genital–genital rubbing to other females) in exchange for food, to become integrated into a group, or simply for the enjoyment of it.

Some scholars feel that bonobo behaviour here is probably much like the sexual behaviour of our pre-human ancestors.[61] Again, this is very different from prosimian behaviour. With the ruffed lemurs, for example, the female refuses any attempted mounts by males until a short period of oestrus during the annual mating season. Here she is receptive to males for only six to eight hours.[62]

But why this difference between the two types of primates? The answer, I would argue, is that it has to do with differences in the complexity of awareness. Anthropoid self-perceptual, interpretive, and cognitive abilities are much more complex than those of prosimians. Chimpanzees and orangutans, for example, are able to recognize themselves in a mirror; prosimians are not.[63] In this view, the sexual desire of non-human anthropoids is tied to awareness in a way that the sexual desire of prosimians is not. Anthropoid sexual desire is thus not fully dependent on hormones in the way that prosimian sexual desire is. Since human beings show an even greater complexity of awareness than do non-human anthropoids, it is only reasonable to assume that human sexual desire will be even less dependent on hormones than is the sexual desire of the other anthropoids.

That human sexual desire operates in a distinct way from the more hormone-dependent sexuality of the other primates is also suggested by the existence of the atypical sexual variations, for example, exhibitionism, voyeurism, fetishism, sadomasochism, and necrophilia. Nothing resembling these human sexual desires can be found in any of the non-human primates.[64] And this is true even for such primates who have had abnormal or abusive upbringings; something the primatologist Dixson feels accounts for atypical sexual desires in human beings.

The likely explanation for this difference is that human sexual desire involves a complex ability to create a system of associative and symbolic meanings that is only rudimentary in other primate's sexual desire. It is this complexity of awareness that enables the atypical sexual variations to appear in human beings.

The overall conclusion, then, can only be that research on the relation between sex hormones and sexual desire has failed to provide any solid evidence that sexual desire is, in any fundamental sense, dependent on the fluctuations of sex hormones. This in turn shows that, since the actions of sex hormones seem the most likely candidate for a biological mechanism that gives rise to the experience of sexual desire, there is little convincing evidence that sexual desire has its basis in our biology.

THE PHENOMENOLOGY OF SEX HORMONES

None of this means, however, that sex hormones bear no relation to sexual desire, but only that they bear no essential role. But what other sort of relation could there be between sex hormones and sexual desire? I mentioned earlier that sexual desire can be roused by stimulation of the erotogenic zones, and especially the sex organs. Given that sex hormones primarily target the genitals and reproductive system, a possible relation is suggested by considering Freud's idea of what he calls the three sources of excitation. According to Freud the sexual apparatus can be set in motion from three sources: excitations of the erotogenic zones from something in the external world, excitations by the interior of the body, or by excitations caused by fantasy.[65] Because some people might be worried by a reference to Freud here, it is perhaps worthwhile to point out that this view that was borrowed by Masters and Johnson and re-named as exteroceptive, proprioceptive, and psychological stimulations.[66]

What Freud is saying is that sexual desire can be roused in three different ways, none of which is necessary but each of which can be sufficient. That is, sexual desire can be roused by merely receiving stimulation from one of these three sources. An example of the first source of excitation would be a caress on an erotically sensitive area of the body by the hand of an attractive member of the desired gender. Perhaps not only the touch, but also the sight, sound, smell, and taste of a desired person should be included in this category; for these are also ways in which something in the external world excites sexual desire. An example of excitation by fantasy could be imagining a romantic or sexual interaction with a person who one finds sexually attractive.[67]

But what about excitations by the interior of the body? Here, I should like to suggest, is where sex hormones have their non-essential relation to sexual desire. That is, sex hormones are one of the sources of excitations by the interior of the body that may or may not lead to sexual desire. Others such sources include muscle tension and movements, and vasocongestion. However, excitations caused by sex hormones are not necessary for sexual desire. This is because, first, they are only one form of excitation from the interior of the body and, secondly, interior excitations are only one of the factors that can lead to sexual desire.

But how then do they lead to sexual desire? The answer, it is clear, will not have to do with biological mechanisms of sex hormones, but rather with the phenomenology of their excitations. That is, the way in which they might lead to sexual desire will depend on the way in which the excitations are dealt with in a person's awareness. This, of course, is a matter for empirical investigation and so should be addressed by phenomenological research. I want to propose a way in which these excitations might relate to sexual desire, and so indicate a possible route for phenomenological investigation.

Sex hormones would seem to play a role in sexual desire because of sensory receptors in the genitals. These are both a main erotogenic zone and are sensitive to the fluctuations of sex hormones. Receptors in the breasts—also typical erotogenic zones in women—are likewise sensitive to fluctuations of sex hormones, namely oestrogen.[68] As Davidson et al. suggest, sex hormones might operate by acting on such receptors or by lowering the threshold for genital sensation.[69] In either case sex hormones work to increase genital excitations. This increase in excitations, I would argue, enters awareness by directing attention to the genitals. In this way, either new sensations or sensations that might have slipped by full awareness before—the pressure of clothing, the rhythmic movement of the legs, and the pulsation of blood vessels—now move forward to situate themselves in clear view before awareness.

In doing so, however, these genital sensations do not proclaim themselves to be elements essentially imbued with erotic meaning. Rather, they enter awareness undeciphered, calling upon awareness to organize them in terms of a specific meaning. This is not to say that in their initial presentation to awareness that they are devoid of meaning, but only that in the moment they appear diverse meanings are already competing to be assigned to them. It is in this state of shifting meanings that they present themselves to awareness as being in need of a specific meaning. In this situation they may either be given or denied an erotic meaning.

This, of course, is just what happens in the case of excitations from objects in the external world. These too are open to the acceptance of diverse meanings. The fact that genital excitations from external objects need not lead to sexual desire is evident from what goes on in medically-based genital exams. Although such exams cause genital stimulation, they do not usually lead to the patient's having sexual desire. This, however, remains a possibility.[70] And just as external excitation of the genitals may or may not lead to sexual desire, so too the interior stimulation of these receptors by sex hormones may or may not lead to sexual desire.

Still, there is a basic difference between excitations caused by external objects and those caused by the interior of the body. In the former case our awareness typically senses not only the excitations themselves, but also the external object that is their cause. Thus, for example, in being caressed by the hand of a person I am sexually attracted to, what I am aware of is not only the excitations on or tingling under the skin where I am caressed, but also the hand (and the body to which it belongs) that is doing the caressing. These are not experienced distinctly, but are rather experienced as a unified and interwoven system in which the hand seems to fuse with my body, penetrating below my skin to mingle with the sensations it has caused. This is precisely what happens, though on a larger scale, in the phenomenology of sexual intercourse. Here, through the penetration of intercourse, both bodies seem to pour into and fuse with each other, giving rise to the experience of an interpenetrating two-body Gestalt.[71]

Things, however, are different with excitations whose origin is the interior of the body. Here there is typically no external object that awareness senses and attempts to associate causally with the bodily sensations. That is, excitations from the interior of the body are left to present themselves alone to awareness. But in presenting themselves alone such excitations are disposed to take on numerous and diverse meanings, none of which need be erotic. This is because there is no external object (for example, a sexually attractive person) that helps to enforce the erotic meaning of the internal excitations. Of course, even excitations caused by the caress of a sexually attractive person need not be construed in an erotic way. But in this case, it seems that an erotic construal is much more likely than in this latter case. Awareness here is filled with an excitation whose erotic meaning seems to press itself in on awareness from several directions at once.

For example, in the moment of a caress on an erotogenic zone of my body by someone I find attractive, not only do I experience the excitations caused by the physical contact but, typically, I also experience the sight, sound, smell, and maybe even taste of the attractive person. If sex hormones are also released in this instance, then not only am I infiltrated with excitations caused from the exterior of my body, but also with those from the interior of the body. There is, so to speak, a double barrage of excitations on the body.

What then happens when excitations from the interior of the body appear alone in awareness? I would argue that just what meaning they are given will depend both on the situation in which they are experienced and also on the dispositions of the person undergoing them. It seems likely that a person in an obviously sexual situation—for example, waiting on one's sexual partner in order to have sexual intercourse—will tend to interpret increased genital sensitivity or excitations, which are the physiological effects of sex hormones, as being related to sexual desire. However, a person experiencing a similar increase in genital sensitivity in a typically non-sexual situation—for example, waiting in a queue at the bank—will tend less to interpret the excitations in a sexual way. Perhaps the excitations will even be ignored. This much seems consistent with attribution theory.[72]

A similar point can be made with a person's dispositions. For example, Kaplan—and Vātsyāyana long before her—distinguishes persons in terms of their degrees of sexual desire, with some being high in sexual desire, some being low, and some being on a gradient of degrees in between. A person's placing here can also be situationally specific, for example, he or she might be low in sexual desire because of a lack of attraction to his or her partner.[73] With increased genital sensitivity it seems probable that a person with a high degree of sexual desire will be more disposed than someone with a low degree to see the excitations as being related to sexual desire.

Likewise, some people may be more sensitive to context than others. Thus, in the right context, namely a clearly sexual one they might not be affected much by a decline in internal excitations. Someone else, however, might be less sensitive and so be more dependent on excitations from the interior of the body. In the same way, it is understandable that someone with a high degree of sexual desire might not respond to the decline of sex hormones in the way that someone would with a low degree of sexual desire. In the case of the person with a high degree of sexual desire internal excitations could serve to heighten his or her desire but not play a very important role. Consequently, a decline in the internal excitation would not have much of an effect on his or her sexual desire. In this case, excitations from the external world and fantasy could be more than enough to set his or her desire in motion. A person with low sexual desire, however, could well find that the lowered amount of internal excitations is enough to herald a decline in his or her already weak desires.

That personal dispositions or sensitivity might play a role here is suggested by what we know about another apparent relation between hormones and experience. Premenstrual syndrome—a syndrome in which a woman shows mood swings at particular times in her menstrual cycle—seems to be related to fluctuations in oestrogen or progesterone levels. However, only women with a history of menstrual cycle-related mood disorder show any change in mood according to such hormone fluctuations.[74] Consequently, whether or not a fluctuation in these hormones leads to a change in moods depends entirely on the dispositions of the woman having the fluctuations.

These possible effects of sex hormones on sexual desire (through the awareness of internal excitations), must be seen within the context of a wider account of multiple influences on sexual desire. There are numerous personal and social factors that could also play roles here. The internal excitations caused by sex hormones are thus but one more factor that may or may not affect sexual desire.

One of the things that make the biological view about sexual desire attractive is that it firmly ties sexual desire to our bodily nature. This is attractive because it underlines the essential connection between sexuality and the body. And plainly, a crucial element in sexual desire is the body; for it is the mutual baring and caressing of bodies that is the decisive object of sexual desire.[75] Yet, one can easily acknowledge this essential role of the body in sexual desire without accepting the biological view, namely the view that sexual desire has its origins in the biological processes of the body. This is because the body is an element in sexual desire only by virtue of the meaning we bestow upon it.

4
Social Constructionism and Sexual Desire

THE SOCIAL CONSTRUCTIONIST MODEL OF SEXUALITY

Many scholars who reject biological essentialism about sexual desire argue instead that sexual desire is somehow culturally or socially constructed. Such a view of sexual desire is based on a more general theory of human existence known as cultural or social constructionism. According to this theory, most if not all aspects of human behaviour and experience are constructed by the culture in which they exist.

In this essay, however, I shall argue that social constructionist accounts of sexual desire are, like biological essentialist accounts, fundamentally flawed and hence that they too are unable to explain sexual desire. This will, no doubt, seem a bewildering conclusion for most scholars working in this area. This is because these two positions are often seen to be not only mutually exclusive but also jointly exhaustive. That is, many people think that these are the only two possible explanations for where sexual desire comes from: either it is biologically based or culturally based (or perhaps a mixture of the two). This is just the nature versus nurture dichotomy applied to the question of sexual desire. There is, however, as I shall try to show, a third alternative. This alternative, which I call the phenomenological view, explains sexual desire as having its origin in the nature of the awareness of our gendered human condition. But before I come to this alternative explanation, let us have a look at the social constructionist account.

We can start by noting that, as Stevi Jackson, Juliet Richters, Carol S. Vance, and others have pointed out, there is little agreement surrounding the exact nature of social constructionism or which theories are to be counted as social constructionist.[1] A measure of order has been placed on the situation by Vance, who, discussing anthropology and sexuality, first contrasts social constructionism with what she calls the cultural influence model and then points to the varying degrees of social constructionist theories.

The cultural influence model, says Vance, "recognizes variations in the occurrence of sexual behaviour and in cultural attitudes which encourage or restrict behaviour, but not in the meaning of the behaviour itself." Social constructionist models, on the other hand, "all reject trans-historical and transcultural definitions of sexuality and suggest instead that sexuality is mediated by historical and cultural factors."[2]

This common basis for social constructionist models finds varying degrees of expression. Thus, concerning social constructionist views of sexual desire, Vance suggests there is a minimal view where the social construction is seen to involve merely the meaning of the desire or behaviour which it motivates. In this view sexual desire itself exists independently of social constructions. According to a stronger but still moderate view, however, it is not just the meaning of sexual desire that is socially constructed, but also the directions which the desire takes. Here, sexual orientation is also seen to be something which is constructed or decided by culture.

In the most radical view, says Vance, "there is no essential, undifferentiated sexual 'impulse,' or 'sex drive,' or 'lust,' which resides in the body due to physiological functioning and sensation. Sexual desire, then, is itself only constructed by culture and history from the energies and capacities of the body."[3] In other words, sexual desire only comes into existence, and takes the particular form it has, because culture and "history" have dictated it should be so.

Unfortunately, Vance herself creates some problems with her classification. It is not clear, for example, how the cultural influence model fundamentally differs from the two non-radical views of social constructionism. Vance tells us that while the social constructionist models recognize variations in the meaning of a behaviour, the cultural influence model does not. But the only attempt to explain what she means by this purported aspect of the cultural influence model comes in her claim that when scholars investigating a culture report on "the presence or absence of 'homosexuality' or 'sexual permissiveness', they engage in a spurious translation from sexual act or behaviour to sexual meaning and identity."[4]

But I fail to see how to report on the presence of homosexuality in a culture is to engage in a translation of the meaning of the behaviour. For simply to report that homosexual acts occur within a culture is not to say anything about the meaning such acts have for the participants or for the culture. In one culture such acts may be considered shameful or deviant, while in another they may be considered essential for biological development. Merely to report the presence of such acts says nothing about their meaning. Such reporting can thus hardly be considered a "spurious translation" of their meaning.

There are also further problems with Vance's attempt to distinguish between the so-called cultural influence model and her account of the two weaker versions of social constructionism. These become evident when she tries to argue that some investigators mistakenly think that the cultural influence and social constructionist models are compatible. Here, she says, "some have assimilated terms or phrases (like 'social constructionism' or 'cultural constructionism') in their work, yet their analytic frames still contain many unexamined essentialist elements."[5]

But on her own account the two weaker views of social constructionism also contain "essentialist elements." It is only with the radical view of social constructionism that all such elements are supposed to have disappeared—which is why it is inconsistent for her to assert, in the same breath, that "all [social constructionist models] reject trans-historical and transcultural definitions of sexuality." For plainly the minimal and moderate views, with their essentialist elements, do not make such a wholesale rejection.

Because of all this I do not not feel that the two weaker views are properly called social constructionist views of sexual desire. For the core object under investigation here—namely sexual desire—is not itself, according to these views, a social construct. It is therefore misleading, if not simply wrong, to say they are social constructionist views of sexual desire.

This view is in agreement with Jacobsen's claim that "social constructionism need not deny biological realities; more plausibly, it often contends that what qualifies as sexual desire emerges only after our biological urges are subject to socialization."[6] The important thing to see here is that in making this assertion about social constructionism and sexual desire, Jacobsen is not qualifying his claim by using the term "radical social constructionism." Rather he is simply making a statement about unqualified social constructionism and sexual desire. A corollary of this would be that if someone holds the view that sexual desire is there independently of the process of social construction, then that view is not accurately called a social constructionist view of sexual desire. This does not imply, however, that scholars holding the radical view hold it consistently. Many self-proclaimed social constructionists are not even clear about which of the supposed degrees of social constructionism they are arguing for. Thus it is common enough to find scholars presenting what looks like the radical view, only to find the evidence they adduce for such a view to be little more than evidence for something like the minimal view.

A good example here can be found in Jackson's work where we are told that:

> sexuality is not definable as a fixed object of analysis. It encompasses all those acts, desires, identities, and relationships understood as in some sense erotic—but the erotic itself is a fluid concept. What is deemed erotic varies across cultures, historical eras and social contexts; what one person finds erotic another might find distasteful, morally unacceptable, or simply boring; the enactment of one person's erotic desires can entail coercive acts towards others (who experience those acts as anything but erotic). What is erotic, and hence sexual, depends on what is defined as such, by whom, in specific social contexts—hence the very definition of the sexual is a social act.[7]

The confusion here should be obvious. For although we are told that sexuality is not definable as a fixed object and that what is sexual is simply decided by a social definition—which is the radical view of social constructionism—the evidence given for these claims is only evidence for the minimal view. For the fact that people have different sexual tastes, or respond with moral indignation to other persons' sexual tastes, does not show that erotic or sexual desire does not exist independently of social definitions. It shows only that different cultures, historical eras, or people assign different meanings to different types of sexual desires.

This is obvious from the fact that seeing a sexual desire as being distasteful, morally unacceptable, or boring is perfectly compatible with still seeing it as being a sexual desire. To find someone else's sexual desire distasteful is not to redefine it as not being a sexual desire; it is merely to see it as a sexual desire that one personally finds distasteful. Indeed, it is not uncommon for people to find their *own* sexual desires distasteful or morally unacceptable.[8] This does not somehow magically turn their sexual desires into non-sexual desires.

FOUCAULT'S TRANSFORMATION OF DESIRE

Much of the problem here can be traced back to Michel Foucault, a thinker whose work is frequently cited as supporting the social constructionist view of sexuality.[9] Tiefer, for example, asserts that "sexuality is created, not just shaped, within the sociocultural movement," while citing Foucault approvingly[10] (see also Jackson; Kimmel; Seidman).[11] The difficulty is that Foucault's work is itself deeply confused. For although he wants to argue that social and historical forces do not simply modify or direct sexual desire but actually create and constitute it, his arguments depend on the idea that sexual desire is something that exists independently of such forces. That is, he too relies on something like the minimal view even though he tries to put forward the radical view. This is probably because, as Morrow suggests, "Foucault at some level is aware of the danger of an anti-realist stance [that is, the radical view] for his own views . . . Like probably all social constructionists he smuggles realist assumptions into his account in order to remain viable."[12]

Thus, although Foucault's premises contain numerous claims about how various historical and cultural factors affect sexual desire, his basic arguments clearly imply that sexual desire has an existence independent of cultural diktats. Here culture is something that merely gets us to discourse about or modify sexual desire, not something that creates or constitutes it. Thus, in arguing that Western history involved an "incitement to discourse" concerning all things sexual, Foucault says that in the seventeenth century "an imperative was established: not only will you confess to acts contravening the law, but you will seek to transform your desire, your every desire into discourse."[13]

But to transform desire in this way is not to create it. Indeed, in order to transform desire into discourse, there must first be a desire there to transform. Likewise, Foucault says, "This is the essential thing: that Western man has been drawn for three centuries to the task of telling everything concerning his sex . . . and that this carefully analytical discourse was meant to yield multiple effects of displacement, intensification, reorientation, and modification of desire Itself."[14] But again, "desire itself" is something that exists independently of these multiple effects. In order for a modification of desire to occur, there must first be a desire there to be modified.

All of this is explicit in Foucault's discussion of what he calls the repressive hypothesis and *scientia sexualis*. However, when he begins to discuss the relation of sexual desire to power (power being something society wields through the beliefs and actions of its members), he then suggests that power and sexual desire are linked in a complex and primary way. He attempts to support this by saying:

> Power is essentially what dictates its law to sex. Which means first of all that sex is placed by power in a binary system: licit and illicit, permitted and forbidden. Secondly, power prescribes an "order" for sex that operates at the same time as a form of intelligibility; sex is to be deciphered on the basis of it relation to the law. And finally, power acts by laying down the rule: power's hold on sex is maintained through language, or rather through the act of discourse it creates, from the very fact that it is articulated, a rule of law.[15]

After making these remarks, Foucault then begins to discuss sexual desire as though he has somehow shown that it is not merely modified by social power, but is rather constituted by such power. Thus a few pages later he suddenly announces that "the law constitutes desire."[16] But where does this conclusion come from? Nothing of what he says earlier shows that sexual desire is, in any fundamental sense, created or constituted by cultural prescriptions. All he has given evidence for is something resembling the minimal view of social constructionism. It might well be that, as he mentions in his first point, culture uses its power to dictate which sex acts or desires are to be considered "permitted and forbidden", but this is entirely compatible with sexual desire having its origins independently of such diktats.

Again, it looks as though sexual desires must first exist in order for culture to decide which acts are to be permitted and which are to be forbidden. The same is true concerning Foucault's second point: to decipher sex or sexual desire in terms of its relation to the law there must be something there to be deciphered in the first place. Of course, such prescriptions or deciphering might well influence sexual desire in various ways. But this is a non-radical view of social constructionism, not the purported radical one. His final point is merely about how *power* works (through the act of discourse it creates), and therefore says nothing about the origin of sexual desire itself.

Because of this, and because of the central role that Foucault plays in social constructionist thinking, it is understandable that social constructionist theorizing is plagued with difficulties.

SCRIPTS WITHOUT A SCRIPTWRITER

The extent of the difficulties here becomes even more noteworthy when it is seen that similar problems can be found in the writings of two other major social contructionists who work in the area of sexuality. The persons I have in mind are Simon and Gagnon.[17] These scholars are important thinkers here because their account of what they call "scripting theory" is heavily relied upon by numerous other sexual theorists who see themselves as being, in some sense, radical social constructionists (for example, Kimmel; Seidman).[18] Such thinkers employ scripting theory as the principal way of explaining how various aspects of sexuality are socially constructed.

But why is scripting theory so popular with social constructionists? This is probably because in scripting theory we get one of the few attempts to spell out the mechanism through which culture does not merely give meaning to or direct our sexual desires and behaviours, but actually creates them. It is true that many of those taking the weaker views of social constructionism also use scripting theory, but I think that Jackson is right when she says that "Gagnon and Simon's position is thoroughly anti-essentialist."[19] This is also the view taken by Richter, who calls their position "a thorough-going social constructionist position."[20]

Simon and Gagnon's position is therefore an expression of the radical view, what I am calling social constructionism proper. In their view, the way in which sexual desire is created is through the mechanism of employing scripts. Simon and Gagnon tell us that "Scripts are essentially a metaphor for conceptualizing the production of behaviour within social life."[21] For behaviour to occur, they say, something resembling scripting must occur at three different levels, namely cultural scenarios, interpersonal scripts, and intrapersonal scripts.

Cultural scenarios, they tell us, are "the instructional guides that exist at the level of collective life." All institutions and institutionalized arrangements can be seen as the systems that dictate these scenarios. Such "guides," however, are not always predictive of an individual's behaviour and are too abstract to be consistently applicable. It is therefore necessary to invoke the further notion of interpersonal scripts. At this level scripts refer to the individual's "improvisation and tinkering" that is often necessary to apply the abstract scenario to the concrete situation.

The possibility of and sometimes necessity for creating such improvisational scripts, say Simon and Gagnon, transforms the individual from being a mere actor into being a "partial scriptwriter."[22] When, however, complexities become rife at the cultural scenario level, then, we are told, interpersonal scripting, which is inadequate to deal with the demands placed on the person, is supplemented by intrapersonal scripting; that is, by an "internal rehearsal" of other possible outcomes. This "internal dialogue" then creates a distinct version of the self and, consequently, the "private world of wishes and desires that are experienced as originating in the deepest recesses of the self must be bound to social life."

Turning to the idea of sexual scripts, Simon and Gagnon say, "the very concept of the scripting of sexual behaviour implies a rejection of the idea that the sexual represents a very special, if not unique quality of motivation."[23] (Although Simon and Gagnon use the term "the sexual" generally to refer, as far as I can see, to various sexual phenomena, they seem mainly to use it to refer to sexual behaviour and sexual desire or motivation.) Sexual behaviour or desire only becomes significant if it is socially defined as significant. Although a person's own experiences might give sexual behaviour or desire significance, any divergence from the prevailing cultural scenarios will "tend to be limited by a universe largely created by such cultural scenarios." Simon and Gagnon conclude that "the motivation to perceive and respond in sexual terms, then, needs to be determined exclusively by what is essential to a given setting." And what is essential will be determined by those cultural scenarios that deal with sexual phenomena:

> Such cultural scenarios not only specify appropriate objects, aims, and desirable qualities of self-other relations but also instruct in times, places, sequences of gesture and utterance and, among the most important, what the actor and his or her coparticipants (real or imagined) are assumed to be feeling; qualities of instruction that make most of us far more committed and rehearsed at the time of our initial sexual encounters than most of us realize.[24]

One peculiar aspect about this theory is that it rests entirely on a metaphor; namely the metaphor of scripts written by a playwright. That is, the metaphor is not just one that is used briefly to illustrate a point; rather it is the very substance of the theory. Thus the ideas of scripts, actors, roles, rehearsals, performances, improvising, entrances, exits, staging, and numerous other concepts from the theatrical world are continually used throughout Simon and Gagnon's account as ways of explaining why people have the desires they do and behave the way they do.

Unfortunately, however, the scripting metaphor, upon which the entire theory turns, only applies in a vague and incomplete way to the phenomena that it is meant to explain. Consequently, since the theory is nothing more than an application of the scripting metaphor, it offers only a vague and incomplete—and therefore inadequate—explanation of what it is meant to explain.

To see this, one need simply note that although the theory presents persons in everyday life as though they were actors acting out various scripts, there are crucial differences between a person in everyday life and an actor on stage reciting his script. For one thing, actors lead distinct lives from the roles they present on stage or before the camera. For example, in the film *Repulsion* the lead character Carol Ledoux slowly goes mad and slashes someone to death with a razor. However, Catherine Deneuve, the actress who plays Carol Ledoux, has not, as far as I know, gone mad or slashed anyone to death with a razor. Therefore, Catherine Deneuve lives a life distinct from that of her role as Carol Ledoux.

On scripting theory, however, there is no person who is distinct from his or her role. There is no one who, like the real actor, at last finishes his or her role and gets off the stage. (The idea of a "social self" that is created out of its social roles, an idea which comes essentially from William James and G. H. Mead, is one which I have elsewhere rejected as untenable.[25]) That scripting theory does not recognize a person who is distinct from the roles being played is what one would expect. If the theory did admit of a person who was no longer acting out a script, there would be a dimension of human existence—an extremely significant one at that—to which scripting theory could no longer apply. And if this were the case, then the idea that human behaviour and desires could be adequately accounted for by notions like cultural scenarios and interpersonal and intrapersonal scripting would be false. But just because scripting theory does not admit of someone who exists behind his or her roles, it cannot be a metaphor of real scripting. For what happens in real scripting, scripting as it is carried out in the world of drama, is that there is someone—an actor—who has a life that is distinct from the role he is playing.

This is not to say that people in everyday life do not sometimes behave as though they were acting, but only that in attempting to reduce every moment of human existence to "something resembling scripting" Simon and Gagnon have cut their theory free from the very concept upon which it is based. This might all be well and good if it were not for the fact that in doing so they have also cut it free from making any sense. For the concept of scripts and acting fundamentally depends upon the idea that there is a difference between the person and the stage character the person is portraying. If either of these elements is removed—the person or the stage character—then what we are left with cannot plausibly be referred to as scripts or acting or even a metaphor of scripts or acting.

Even in the case where we say that someone in everyday life (rather than in the theatrical world) is acting, we still mean—and must mean for our claim to make sense—that there is some sort of difference between the person and the behaviour he is displaying. This is captured in our saying, as we often do in such cases, that the person is not being himself, is being false or affected, is putting on a show, or some such thing. However, once it is denied that there are two distinct entities here, then the concept of acting or performing a script can no longer be intelligibly applied. It should also be noted that the idea of there being an entity that is behind or is distinct from the role being played does not imply the existence a persisting and immutable self, but only that behind the acting-like behaviour there is a distinct awareness which is not reducible to the awareness portrayed in the behaviour.[26]

Such is the obviousness of this problem that, despite their claims about the non-existence of a self or person behind the roles being played, Simon and Gagnon are themselves compelled to introduce just such an entity. This is the entity that does the "tinkering" with the cultural scenarios in order to create interpersonal scripts and therefore is himself or herself a "partial scriptwriter". For in being a scriptwriter (and it is irrelevant here whether he is a partial or full scriptwriter) the person is no longer acting out a script but is rather creating one. And here we thus have a dimension of human existence—the writing of a script—where a person's thoughts, desires, and behaviour take place outside the realm of scripts, and consequently a dimension of human existence for which scripting theory can no longer account.

Of course, Simon and Gagnon might try to claim that the person's act of scriptwriting is also itself scripted. But what kind of script could this be? It could not be a script of a cultural scenario; for the scriptwriting here is undertaken precisely because cultural scenarios, being too abstract, are no longer applicable. It could not be an interpersonal script; for interpersonal scripts require that the person performing them is himself partially responsible for writing them. And if the act of partial scriptwriting is itself scripted, and the person involved in the partial scriptwriting is also responsible for the scripting of the act of partial scriptwriting, then we have an infinite regress where each scripting of the previous script requires a further scriptwriting, and so on *ad infinitum*.

The only remaining option would be that the partial scriptwriting of the interpersonal script is itself scripted at the level of intrapersonal scripting.

But this will not do either, because by its very definition intrapersonal scripting only takes place when interpersonal scripting is inadequate to deal with the demands placed on the person. That is, intrapersonal scripting is a response to the failure of interpersonal scripting, not an element in its creation.

Simon and Gagnon's awareness that the idea of "partial scriptwriter" is a spanner in the works of their theory becomes evident when, in turning to sexual scripts, they tell us that although a person might display deviations from prevailing cultural scenarios (that is, partial scriptwriting), any divergence here will "tend to be limited by a universe largely created by such cultural scenarios". For with this it is clear that they hope to deal with the contradiction at the heart of their theory by removing even more of the person's own contribution to his own desires. Here the person is no longer merely a "partial scriptwriter", but now a "limited partial scriptwriter".

But this manoeuvre is of no help; because just as it does not matter whether the person is a partial rather than a full scriptwriter, likewise it does not matter whether the person is a partial rather than a limited partial scriptwriter. In each case there still exists a person or awareness behind the scripts whose actions or desires—no matter how limited or partial they are—cannot be fully explained by the idea of scripting.

Again, Simon and Gagnon seem aware of this continued inconsistency in their account and so at last are forced to contradict their earlier claims and, forgetting about the limited partial scriptwriter, assert that the motivation to think and act in sexual terms is "*determined exclusively* by what is essential to a given setting" (emphasis added), and that what is essential will be determined by sexual cultural scenarios that "not only specify appropriate objects, aims, and desirable qualities of self-other relations but also instruct in times, places, sequences of gesture and utterance" and so on. But this goes completely against their own idea that cultural scenarios are, by themselves, inadequate to explain human actions.

The main problem, then, seems to be that Simon and Gagnon want it both ways: in one way they want cultural scenarios to explain all human desires and behaviour, but in another way they want to be true to the facts and allow that cultural scenarios cannot explain everything. As a result, they are compelled to introduce the ideas of interpersonal and intrapersonal scripting that are supposed to enable divergence from cultural scenarios because they are "written" (partially) by the person. But this person is nevertheless writing "exclusively" under the influence of cultural scenarios. Consequently, scripting theory cannot help but collapse into a tangle of contradictions.

From the foregoing it should be clear that there is far more confusion attending the social constructionist view of sexual desire than is generally seen. Although some people might want to take this as support for biological essentialism, as was shown in the last essay, this view is also beset with difficulties. A rejection of both these positions might seem strange to those who see biological essentialism and social constructionism as being jointly exhaustive accounts of the origin of sexual desire. But as I mentioned this is a false dichotomy: for there is at least one other alternative. This is the view that sexual desire has its origin in existential features of human awareness.

THE PHENOMENOLOGICAL VIEW OF SEXUAL DESIRE

It is true, of course, that awareness is dependent on the brain, and that the brain is part of human biology. But this does not mean that the phenomenological view, as I call it, is really a form of biological essentialism. For here biological essentialism is normally understood to be the view that sexual desire is a biological drive that is under the sway of genetic codes, the fluctuation of sex hormones, or some such biological mechanism. In the phenomenological view, however, sexual desire appears because of the way that awareness responds to its existential situation.

This view is in full agreement with the social constructionist claim, as given by Vance that "there is no essential, undifferentiated sexual 'impulse,' or 'sex drive,' or 'lust,' which resides in the body *due to physiological functioning and sensation*" (emphasis added). However, it goes against the social constructionist conclusion, as given by Vance, that "sexual desire, then, is itself only constructed by culture and history from the energies and capacities of the body." This is because the response of awareness here has little to do with social constructions. In other words, the rejection of biological essentialism does not imply the acceptance of social constructionism.

But how does sexual desire arise from the response of awareness to its existential situation? This is, of course, an empirical question and therefore one that needs to be addressed by phenomenological research. Here, however, I want again to suggest a possible view that might help to direct such research. This view starts with the observation that a fundamental element of human existence is the awareness that one has a gender, which I suggested in the first essay is based on anatomical sex. There are numerous other elements in human existence, but the awareness of being a particular gender seems a fundamental one in most if not all cultures.[27] But to be aware that one has a particular gender is, at the same time, to have the sense that one is lacking in what is experienced as another gender.

And this is so even in the case of intersexuality. For to be truly intersexual is to show a mixture of male and female sexual anatomy. But to show such a mixture is, as I argued in the first essay, to be neither fully male nor female. Consequently, the intersexual person is, just like males and females, also lacking in gender. The difference is that the intersexual person is lacking in two genders whereas the male or female is only lacking in one. Again, as I mentioned in that essay, some intersexual conditions still allow the person to be one gender. Further, it is not only in the awareness of one's own gender that one senses this lack of another gender, but also in the awareness of the other person's gender. For here too, in being aware of the other person's, say, female gender, I am at the same time aware that she is not a male.

This implies that an integral aspect of the awareness of gender is a sense of incompleteness or emptiness. The idea that the experience of emptiness is basic to human awareness is one that numerous thinkers, from Lao-tzu to Sartre, have argued for.[28] In the awareness of gender, I want to suggest, this experience of emptiness is fundamentally connected to sexual desire. This is because sexual desire is experienced as the desire to incorporate into one's body another gender while at the same time having one's own gender enter into the desired person's body, either in reality or in fantasy, in such a way as to fill out the emptiness that is sensed as a central feature of both one's own gender and the gender of the desired person. This is what I argued in Essay 3 that the sexual positions allow us to do in various ways.

Something like this is suggested in ancient Chinese Taoist writings on sexuality.[29] Here the female's sexual energy or *yin* is seen to be balanced or filled out by the male's sexual energy or *yang*, and the same is true of *yang* with regard to *yin*, which is not to say that only males have *yang* and only females have *yin*. Sexual interaction is thus seen as a comingling in which both *yin* and *yang* receive what they lack through an intimate blending.

This is why, according to the phenomenological view, sexual interaction typically involves engaging the genitals, both one's own and those of the other person.[30] For it is just these features of the body that constitute the genders of the persons involved. Even in those instances of sexual interaction that do not involve the genitals—say erotic kissing or fondling non-genital regions of the body—an awareness of the genitals (that is, the gender) of the other person still seems paramount.

Thus, although a heterosexual woman who is involved in erotically kissing her partner may not be having sexual intercourse or even be in contact with her partner's genitals, it would nevertheless seem to be crucial for her that her partner has male genitals rather than female genitals—this is what it means to be a heterosexual female. There are, of course, sexual desires which seem directed to objects or non-persons, such as in object fetishism or zoophilia. But even though such objects are not human bodies, they nevertheless seem, as I have argued elsewhere, connected in fantasy or symbolism to a human body of a particular gender and therefore to the genitals.[31]

The idea of the other person's gender filling the emptiness in one's own gender or of one's own gender similarly filling the emptiness in the other person's gender is understandable in heterosexual desire. Here, the male, for example, experiences the female as displaying a gender that he himself lacks. As a result he seeks to engage her body in intimate physical contact and, through the mutual baring and caressing of bodies, bring his gender together with hers. For it is this contact that creates the sense of filling the emptiness that he experiences in both their genders. This is sensed as a merging of his gender with hers. And the same is true, with the appropriate changes being made, for the heterosexual female and her desire for sexual interaction with the male.

With homosexual desire, however, things are different. For here what the person desires is to incorporate into his or her body with another instance of gender in which the gender is the same as his or hers. This is because, phenomenologically, the homosexual senses his emptiness in gender as being what Tripp calls "a felt-shortage" of his own gender.[32]

Therefore, in desiring sexual interaction with a person of his own gender, the homosexual is, just like the heterosexual, seeking to incorporate into his own body another gender which he senses will fill the emptiness that is experienced at the core of his gender. Since, as just mentioned, gender is based on sexual anatomy, then here it is the genitals of the same-sexed person that are seen as being the answer to the emptiness of the homosexual's own gender. They become, in the experience of desire, the decisive feature of the person towards whom sexual desire is directed.

This remains true, it should be noted, even in bisexuality. For the bisexual is not indifferent to the gender of the person with whom she desires sexual interaction. In the moment of sexual desire the bisexual, like the heterosexual and the homosexual, also focuses on the gender of the person desired. The difference is simply that unlike the heterosexual or homosexual, the bisexual senses her emptiness in relation to both genders and therefore has the ability to desire sexual interaction with persons of both genders.[33] In each of these orientations sexual desires appears as a response to the experience of gender.

It is important, however, to see that this is not meant to explain why someone ends up with one sexual orientation rather than another, that is, why someone goes onto experience his own gender as primarily lacking one rather than the other gender. Here it might be felt that even though the radical degree of social constructionism has been shown to be confused, the moderate view might be applicable here. On this view, although sexual desire itself is not constructed, the orientation it takes is. Such a version of social constructionism is argued for by Gilbert Herdt in his account of the ritualized homosexuality practiced by the Sambia tribe in Papua New Guinea. I shall explore his account in the next essay. For now I will merely state that the reason why a person's sexual desire ends up taking one direction rather than another is probably something that would be best explained—as Seymour Fisher argues—by the dynamics of the Oedipal triangle.[34]

Therefore, rather than presenting a theory of how sexual orientation is acquired, I am here presenting the phenomenological structure that underlies any particular orientation once it has, for whatever reasons, been acquired.

For it is in this structure that one finds the explanation for why human beings have sexual desire, regardless of which direction their desire takes.

Here, then, one can discern the phenomenlogical structure wherein sexual desire has its origin. This structure involves an awareness of one's own gender, which at the same time involves an awareness of what I have called the emptiness of one's own gender. It also involves an awareness of the other person's gender, which at the same time involves an awareness of the emptiness of the other person's gender. In this structure the element of emptiness makes a double appearance: once in the perception of my own gender and once in my perception of the other person's gender.

If, for example, I am a heterosexual male and the other person, real or fantasized, is a female (*and* I find her sexually attractive—this is where the psychology of individual differences would play a role in the awareness), then my awareness is structured in such a way that I sense my gender as something whose void opens itself out be filled by the other person. At the same time, I also sense that her gender's emptiness reaches out to be filled by my gender, which is not to say that she experiences this. For she might not be attracted to me or even be aware of me. She might, after all, be only an element in my fantasy. It is thus only to say that I experience her gender in this way. This also holds, with the appropriate changes being made, for each gender and each sexual orientation.

What this suggests is that sexual desire has its origins in the experience of gender. Sexual desire arises simply because we are aware of both our own gender and the genders of others, and that gender phenomenologically presents itself to us as something that is empty and thus in need of filling. The gender that presents in this way is, as I argued in the first essay, based on the genitals of the person in question. This awareness, I suggest, is something that is fundamental to the human condition and thus has little to do with social construction.

Just as with the biological view social constructionism also has its attractive aspects. One such aspect is that it seems to acknowledge the humanistic features of our existence by freeing us from biological constraints and placing us within the human world of culture. The problem here, however, is that the same in stroke that we are set free from biology we are also swept up into a prison of cultural dictates. The advancement of the phenomenological theory is that it releases us from both forms of incarceration. On this view, sexual desire is neither created by our biology nor by cultural dictates. It is rather our own response to our human condition. We are still, of course, constrained to respond, but that is part of what it means to be human.

5
Gilbert Herdt on Sambia Sexual Culture

SAMBIA RITUALIZED HOMOSEXUALITY

In the last essay I referred in passing to a so-called "moderate social constructionist" view that saw sexual orientation as being something that is constructed by culture. One such view that has received much attention is Gilbert Herdt's account of the Sambia tribe of the Eastern Highlands of Papua New Guinea.[1] Herdt bases his account on his fieldwork on the Sambia, which is not the tribe's real name but a pseudonym invented by Herdt to help protect the tribe's privacy. Herdt's account of the Sambia's sexual practices and desires is so widely cited and uncritically accepted, that it seems worthwhile to give an in-depth examination of his work and see if his findings support his position.

The aspect of Sambia sexual culture on which Herdt focuses, and the one which has generated the most interest, is the culturally prescribed period of male homosexuality which takes place prior to the Sambia male's heterosexual marriage. Although culturally prescribed homosexuality has long been studied in the various other cultures of Melanesia,[2] Sambia sexual culture has received special attention because Herdt argues that the sexual behaviour of the Sambia shows how profoundly Sambia sexual desires—and thus, by implication, sexual desires in any culture—are conditioned by historical and cultural influences.

Herdt's view is in contrast to those of many of the earlier Melanesian ethnographers. These scholars saw such homosexual activity as being merely "institutionalized" or "ritualized" and thus not as being indicative of the participant's actual sexual desires. Herdt, however, argues that the Sambia who engage in the prescribed homosexual activities are not merely doing so because it is ritually prescribed, but are rather doing so because of genuine homosexual desires that their culture has, through "deep scripting", implanted in them. As Sambia boys become young men, their culture then, through similar scripting, gets them to give up their homosexual desires and acquire heterosexual ones. But why does Herdt think all this? To answer this, let us have a close look at Sambia prescribed homosexuality.

This homosexuality involves young boys performing fellatio on older adolescent boys and takes place in a complex web of beliefs concerning female pollution and the masculinizing properties of semen. Sambia, whose culture contains a high amount of antagonism between the genders, believe that a boy must be removed from his mother at about the age of nine in order to avoid female pollution and must start ingesting semen through fellatio.

Although girls are thought to develop naturally into fully functioning women, boys, having no semen of their own, are thought to require the semen of other males to develop. Even though boys are assigned at birth to the male gender because of their genitals, it is believed that they will not be able to produce their own semen without first ingesting the semen of older boys. This ingestion is believed to be essential for developing strong bones and muscles, male secondary sex characteristics, and reproductive competence. Consequently, pre-pubescent Sambia boys perform fellatio on older boys until they themselves reach puberty and, in turn, start themselves being fellated by younger boys.

This sort of homosexual activity, however, comes in most cases to an abrupt halt with the young man's marriage in his late teens or later. Here Sambia culture now prescribes exclusive heterosexual behaviour for the male and his wife (usually involving sexual intercourse, but also heterosexual fellatio).

In appraising Herdt's interpretation of Sambia sexual behaviour is important to note that there is nothing strange about the Sambia sex acts in themselves: the act of fellatio, in either its homosexual or heterosexual forms, is not peculiar to the Sambia. Acts of fellatio of both types are depicted in various art forms throughout the world, discussed in the ancient Indian and Chinese erotic works, and are a common practice in contemporary Western culture.[3]

Likewise, there is nothing odd about the Sambia practice of adult sexual intercourse. Sexual intercourse between adults is practised in all cultures. Thus, what has caused so much interest is not the Sambia sexual acts themselves, but rather the fact that that nearly all Sambia males shift from exclusive homosexual behaviour to exclusive heterosexual behaviour at a culturally prescribed time. If Herdt's interpretation of this shift in behaviour is right, it seems to be a case where a person's—or, to be more precise, a male's—

sexual desires suddenly shift their orientation (from homosexual to heterosexual) according to the prescriptions or "scripts" of his culture. This goes against the view of many sexologists that sexual orientation is not a superficial preference that can be culturally manipulated at various points in a person's life, but is rather a basic part of the individual's psychic constitution that is crystallized in early childhood.[4]

Although it might be tempting to see the Sambia case here as a form of bisexuality—and thus as something which is not too distinct from bisexuality in Western culture—the Sambia case is different in important ways. For bisexual behaviour usually refers to a person's engaging, of his or her own accord, in both heterosexual and homosexual behaviour during the same period of his or her life, typically going back and forth between the two types of activity. In Sambia culture, however, there tends to be a period of exclusive homosexual activities which is then followed by a sudden shift to exclusive heterosexual activity. Further, and more importantly for the current discussion, this shift in sexual activity is something which is culturally prescribed and engaged in by nearly all male members of the culture.

But does such behaviour show that Sambia culture has dictated the orientations that the sexual desires of its males are to take? Herdt thinks so. As he puts it, "Sambia sexual culture fundamentally split apart desires, gendered them, and made sexual practices and sociosexual objects the instrumentality of their culture and power structures."[5] Herdt himself is quite impressed with Sambia sexual practices and says that they unalterably changed his views of sexual desire.

THE DESIRES BEHIND THE RITUALS

A close reading of Herdt's work, however, shows that there is no reason to think that sexual desires of the Sambia are "split apart" and "gendered" by the rituals to which Herdt refers and that any purported influences here come from a biased interpretation on Herdt's part, which has no basis in the data. This is because Herdt's claims about the sexual desires of the Sambia are founded almost exclusively on their sexual behaviour and betray little concern for any non-sexual desires that might motivate the behaviour. But as is well known, sexual behaviour can be engaged in for numerous reasons, many of which have nothing to do with sexual desire.[6] This fact is especially important to be aware of when one is studying the sexual desires of people from a sexually non-permissive and prescriptive culture like that of the Sambia. To get an idea of how Sambia sexual desires might diverge from their sexual behaviour, let us start by examining how Sambia boys are led to their first homosexual practices.

As we have just seen, young Sambia boys are removed, sometimes forcibly, from their mothers. This can involve the wailing of mothers and death threats to the child made by the abducting men. Once taken from their mothers the boys are then beaten with switches, after which they have sharp sticks driven up their noses until they bleed profusely (to remove the female pollution), and are then whipped with stinging nettles. Some of the men then dress the boys in clothing that signals their new status as fellators, while others try to humiliate the boys by laughing at them and making lewd comments and jokes about what they will soon have to do.

Other men appear in warrior paint and costumes playing bamboo flutes which symbolize, among other things, the penis. A man then goes down the line of the boys trying to insert the flute into their mouths and getting them to suck it. Refusal to suck the flute is sometimes met with verbal intimidation, threats (for example, with a machete), and violence (being struck hard with the flute), while a boy's compliance meets much praise and approval.

Despite all of this, about half the boys still refuse to suck the flute. The boys then receive lectures from high-status elders about the importance of performing fellatio and drinking semen for a boy who wants to grow and become strong. They are forbidden to touch or even look at females until they marry and are also threatened with castration if, when they later marry, they sleep with another man's wife.

At this point the boys are then led back to a cult house where costumed older boys, said to be female spirits, dance making sexual gestures before the younger boys as the night approaches. This is done in the presence of older men who once again tell the young boys they must perform fellatio; any remark or noise from the young boys could here provoke a thrashing from the men. These dancers then take the younger boys out on to a darkened dance ground where the younger boys perform fellatio on them. Again, not all the younger boys (and not all the older boys) take part.

It is, of course, hardly noteworthy that a nine-year-old child who is subjected to such coercion, violence, threats, and lectures by authority figures—a procedure which Herdt himself likens to brainwashing—acquiesces to carry out the prescribed activity. What *is* noteworthy is that, despite the bullying and intimidation, some boys are nevertheless able to resist the "sexual practices and sociosexual objects" that are "the instrumentality of their culture and power structures." Further, it is just this patent coerciveness of the entire ritual that should make us suspicious of claims that the homosexual activities performed during or as a result of the ritual in any way reflect the participant's real sexual desires.

Yet in reading Herdt's presentation of the material it is easy to be misled and think that the Sambia boys' sexual activities are representative of their sexual desires. One of the reasons for this is Herdt's choice of terminology to describe the prescribed sexual activity. Thus, instead of referring to their sexual acts as *homosexual* activity, he continually refers to them as *homoerotic* activity or *homoeroticism*.

But as Herdt himself is aware, the term "homoerotic" implies the existence of homosexual desire in a way that the term "homosexual" does not. If, for example, someone is coerced into performing a homosexual act for which he has no sexual desire, it is nevertheless true to say that he engaged in homosexual activity. This is because the term "homosexual activity" signifies merely the nature of the physical activity and need carry no implications with it about the person's desires. If, however, we try to describe the same situation by saying that the coerced person engaged in homo*erotic* activity or showed homo*eroticism*, then we are introducing unwarranted implications into our description, namely that he sexually desired or sexually enjoyed the activity. This is because terms with the root "erotic" imply a connection to sexual desire. In Herdt's own words, the term "erotic" "refers specifically to that which stimulates sexual desire and arousal,"[7] with the term "homoerotic" referring to a person's "preferred, intentional, desire."[8]

Consequently, it is begging the question to refer, as Herdt does, to Sambia prescribed homosexual acts as homoerotic or homoeroticism unless it has already been shown that such acts are based on, connected to, or stimulate sexual desire. But nowhere in all of Herdt's data is this ever shown. What we are given rather is simply descriptions of the Sambia sexual rituals and sexual behaviour. But this is hardly enough to show that the desires which motivate the behaviour are erotic desires. Indeed, the fact that Sambia boys have to be coerced and beaten into performing the homosexual activities required of them, along with the fact that the majority of Sambia males require no coercion to engage later in heterosexual activity, and—despite the high amount of gender antagonism and fears of female pollution—find heterosexual intercourse intensely exciting and pleasurable,[9] clearly suggest that the prescribed childhood and adolescent homosexual acts are not motivated in any great way by homosexual desire.

Herdt is aware of the implications of this problem, saying that no issue has been of greater interest in the anthropology of homosexuality than that of deciding whether such activities can be described in terms of homoeroticism or whether they are not just instances of social conformity (though, with the Sambia, social coercion would be a better term). Yet the most he does to try to respond to this issue of "great interest" is to state "it is a necessary redundancy to say that without sexual excitement—as signified by erections in the inspirer and bawdy enthusiasm in the inspired boy—these social practices would not only lie beyond the erotic, but more elementary, would not exist."[10]

But this argument is fallacious on several accounts. First, it is false that without sexual excitement a social practice would lie beyond the erotic, if by erotic one means (as Herdt does) sexual desire. For, as several researchers have shown, there is no necessary connection between the two: one can have sexual desire without having sexual excitement and one can have sexual excitement without having sexual desire.[11]

Secondly, the fact that a child might show "bawdy enthusiasm" in sexually satisfying an older person is hardly indicative of the child's behaviour being motivated by sexual excitement or desire. As is well known, child victims of adult or adolescent sexual abuse are often willing and even enthusiastic participants in the sexual acts which they are manipulated into performing.[12] Here the motivation is frequently a desire for the adult's approval and love or fear of rejection. In the Sambia context, as we have seen, the children who suck the flute or symbolic penis, and also real penises, are warmly praised and approved of by the adult males. Further, Sambia boys are led to believe that they will not grow into strong men—objects of high regard in Sambia culture—if they do not perform fellatio.

All of this suggests that it is quite unwarranted to interpret the child's enthusiasm in carrying out the act as being indicative of sexual excitement or desire. Lest it be thought that Herdt's view is supported by his further claim that "some" of the older-boy fellators experience erections while performing fellatio, it is important to note that the only example he gives of such a boy is one who, when he grew up, failed to make the prescribed transition to heterosexuality. As a man he never desired or had sexual intercourse with any of his four successive wives (all of whom left him), had a strong aversion to women, and sexually daydreamed about young boys, continuing to seek them out long after Sambia cultural rules dictated he should be exclusively heterosexual.

Moreover, he even broke the strict taboos by reversing the roles and trying himself to perform fellatio on the young boys, all of whom refused and were disturbed or amused by the incident (not, it should be noted, sexually excited by it). In other words, the only example we are given of someone who, as an older-boy fellator, had erections while performing fellatio is someone who is an exclusive homosexual.

But this is uninteresting. What Herdt has to do to support his argument is to give us examples of men who happily made the transition to exclusive heterosexuality but nevertheless had erections earlier while performing fellatio. By not giving even one such example, Herdt only creates suspicions that the rest of the "some" who had such erections—if "some" here means more than one (and it might well not)—were also, like this man, homosexual. It also cannot escape notice here that the childhood of this Sambia exclusive homosexual—with his rejecting and absent father, lack of any male role model, and a mother who resented men and discouraged her son from partaking in male activities—fits remarkably well with psychoanalytic accounts of the genesis of male homosexuality.[13]

A third problem is that although Herdt tells us here that boys performing the fellatio show bawdy enthusiasm, this goes against what he says elsewhere. When initially presenting his data he says "despite great social pressures, some boys evince from the start a low interest, and they seldom participate in fellatio; on the other hand, some novices feverishly join in. Those are the two extremes: the great majority of Sambia boys regularly engage in fellatio for years, as constrained by taboo."[14] This statement makes it clear that, if there is bawdy enthusiasm shown in the performance of fellatio, it is only shown by a minority of boys at the extreme end of the continuum. Consequently, even if we allowed that the child's enthusiasm were acceptable evidence for the existence of sexual desire (which it is not), we would only have evidence for the existence of such desire in a minority of the Sambia boys. It is in just such a minority that one might expect to find those "some" who had erections while performing fellatio.

As for Herdt's claim that the erections signify sexual excitement in the "inspirer" (a question-begging term for an older boy who is receiving fellatio), this too is completely unwarranted. As Kaplan points out, persons with exclusive homosexual desires can learn to become excited and even have orgasms in a heterosexual encounter.[15] And the same is true for heterosexual persons in a homosexual encounter, as often occurs in prison settings.[16] What makes this possible is the use of sexual fantasy. It is because of this that fantasy and desire, rather than behaviour, should be seen as the true indicator of sexual orientation.[17]

Thus, if a heterosexual adolescent boy is fantasizing that the young boy who is performing fellatio on him is a girl, then he might well be able to become sexually excited and have an erection. The fact that young Sambia males are not only forbidden to touch females, but also forbidden to masturbate (along with the fact that the majority accept heterosexuality with open arms when they are at last allowed to), strongly suggest that some such fantasizing is used by the Sambia adolescent.

In Western culture, an adolescent heterosexual male with no sexual access to females typically engages in masturbation while fantasizing about sexual interaction with a girl. There are, of course, other reasons for masturbating too, but this at least is one of them. If such a person who had no access to females were also prohibited from masturbating and, at the same time, coerced into turning to young boys who are readily available to perform fellatio, it might well seem to him that a reasonable solution to his dilemma would be to allow fellatio to be performed on him by the boy while fantasizing he was being fellated by or having sexual intercourse with a girl.

Could not this be exactly what is happening in the Sambia case? This interpretation seems so obvious that it is remarkable that Herdt never considers it. Further, Herdt's data will not let us decide against this interpretation because his data contain no information on whether and to what extent Sambia adolescent males are fantasizing in their sexual encounters with the young boys.

In his own (or perhaps Stoller's) words, his data are "fantasy-impoverished" and thus "not satisfactory."[18]

In the final pages of his book, Herdt at last admits that although he has been "approaching" the question of how erotic ritualized homosexual relations really are, he has also been avoiding it. His reason for doing so, he tells us, is because answering such a question would require the space for an essay unto itself (even though the entire last chapter which deals with just this question is an essay unto itself). Another reason, we are told, is that "the questions raised regarding the erotic aspect require us to venture into philosophical debates: namely, is the personal erotic desire the culturally collective sexual desire."[19]

But what is wrong with venturing into this debate? And if venturing into this debate is required to answer the question, and Herdt has not ventured into it, then plainly he has not answered the question. And if he has not answered the question, then it is misleading for him to imply that he has by calling prescribed homosexual acts "homoeroticism," by making claims about Sambia sexual culture fundamentally splitting apart desires, and by otherwise implying that his work addresses "questions raised regarding the erotic aspect."

None of this is to say that Herdt's research is not useful: it is full of fascinating data, presenting numerous insights and observations. Nor is it to imply that culture does not play a role in determining how and when people carry out their sexual activities. It is, however, to say that nothing in Herdt's work provides a convincing argument for what appears to be his main conclusion, namely that Sambia sexual culture has "fundamentally split apart desires" or dictated the directions they should take. That Sambia sexual culture plays but a minimal role in "scripting" or affecting the sexual desires of the Sambia also follows from the fact that, as I have argued in the previous essay, sexual desire is an existential need that has its origins in the awareness of our gendered condition, a feature that is common to all human beings across all cultures.[20]

MCCONAGHY TO THE DEFENCE

My critique of Herdt's account, however, has been attacked by Nathaniel McConaghy. He says that people need to "acknowledge the evidence questioning the community view that people are either heterosexual or gay." He then goes on to criticize my critique saying that in order to account for the adolescent's sexual arousal, "Giles found it necessary to suggest the older boy may be fantasizing that the younger boy is a girl. However, if the evidence is accepted that 20% of adolescent boys in western culture experience homosexual feelings, it would seem necessary to exclude the possibility that this is equally true of Sambia boys."

He then states that "Giles' . . . conclusion that 'if there is a bawdy enthusiasm shown in the performance of fellatio, it is only shown by a minority of boys at the extreme end of the continuum' . . . seems influenced by the community belief that people capable of homosexual arousal are an extreme minority."[21] He further claims that I suggest that any boy who had erections while performing fellatio "would later become exclusive homosexuals."[22] There are, however, many problems with McConaghy's assertions.

First, it seems that McConaghy is attacking a straw man. Is it really true that the community view is that people are either heterosexual or gay? It seems pretty obvious that most people accept the existence of bisexuality in its varying degrees and, consequently, do not hold the view that all people are either heterosexual or gay. I certainly do not hold this view, as should have been obvious to McConaghy from my discussion of bisexuality.

Secondly, I fail to see how the fact that only 20% of people report having "awareness of *some* homosexual feelings" (my emphasis) means we should abandon the distinction between heterosexuality and homosexuality. This is like arguing that the existence of intersexuality proves that we should abandon the distinction between male and female. Of course, the presence of bisexuality means it is wrong to hold the view that *all* persons are either exclusively heterosexual or homosexual, but it is unlikely that anybody seriously entertains such a view.

Thirdly, although it is an empirical question, I doubt that "the community" holds the view that the terms "heterosexual" and "homosexual" are synonymous with "exclusive heterosexual" and "exclusive homosexual." As Kinsey suggested long ago, there exists a degree of blending of heterosexual and homosexual desires stretching from exclusive heterosexual at one end of the continuum to exclusive homosexual at the other. The existence of this continuum does not mean, however, that a woman in her 40s, for example, who, as a 14-year-old had "some homosexual feelings," but since then has had only heterosexual desires, is not properly considered a heterosexual. This is because the terms "heterosexual" and "homosexual," if I am not mistaken, are normally used to refer to a person's *predominate* orientation, which is why the term "exclusive heterosexual" is not redundant.

Of course, as Kinsey's scale shows, there are areas where it will be unclear whether a person should be considered heterosexual rather than bisexual, or bisexual rather than homosexual, but this hardly shows that the terms "heterosexual" and "homosexual" can only mean "exclusive heterosexual" and "exclusive homosexual."

As for McConaghy's claim that I was influenced by the community view, when I concluded that, if there was bawdy enthusiasm, it was only shown by a minority of the Sambia boys, McConaghy did not notice that I was merely drawing a conclusion from Herdt's own statements. In one place, Herdt tells us that the young Sambia boys show "bawdy enthusiasm" in their performance of fellatio, while in another place he tells us that some boys show little interest from the start, seldom participating, while other boys "feverishly join in." These are, he tells us the two extremes. Most of the boys regularly perform fellatio as they have been instructed to do. Thus, it follows from Herdt's own words that the enthusiasm referred to only occurs at one extreme end of the continuum.

Concerning McConaghy's further assertion that I suggested Sambia boys who have erections while performing fellatio would later become exclusive homosexuals, this is simply false. Nowhere do I say such a thing. What I say is that the only example Herdt gives of a boy fellator who had such erections is of a boy who later became an exclusive homosexual. I point this out to show the paucity and inappropriateness of the data upon which Herdt bases his assertions about the Sambia "scripting" of homosexual desires in the majority of Sambia boys. Because of all this, I do not think McConaghy has presented any grounds for abandoning the heterosexual/homosexual distinction (it never was a dichotomy) or has shown anything to be wrong with my criticisms of Herdt's view of Sambia sexual desires.

6
No Such Thing as Excessive Levels of Sexual Behaviour

THE NEGATIVE VIEW OF SEXUALITY

So far I have explored the nature of gender and sexual desire, the role of gender in sexual desire, and the expression of this desire in the sexual positions. Another related aspect of the expression of sexual desire is the frequency of its expression—that is, the amount of sexual behaviour shown by particular individuals. A common topic here is the question of whether there is such thing as "too much" sexual activity. That is, is there any basis to argue that a person who engages in a particular amount of sexual behaviour, say, per week is engaging in excessive levels of sexual behaviour? This is a topic on which there is much scholarly disagreement. I myself want to examine this question by focusing on a particular study that claims that there is such thing as excessive levels of sexual behaviour and, further, claims to have discovered what counts as excessive levels.

One of the reasons I want to examine this study is because in arguing that there is such a thing as excessive levels of sexual behaviour, the authors are at the same time giving arguments that support conservative moral or religious values. And any a study of sexuality that offers such support is one that should be subjected to scrutiny. This is because the history of writings on sexuality is swarming with moral and religious influences that are forever trying to masquerade as scientific data. It is just these sorts of writings that have, I feel, caused much damage to people's sexual health and well-being. It should be obvious to anyone that in Western culture there is a widely held negative view of human sexuality. Sexuality is seen to be something that is taboo, not to be mentioned, embarrassing, and to be kept hidden, especially from children (though, oddly enough, violence and cruelty are happily given full exposure).

It is true that over the last decades there have been attempts to remedy this, but theses attempts are for the most part not only half-hearted but also disingenuous. Anyone who looks at the typical sex-education syllabus for school-age children, for example, will easily notice that what should be the central topic of the course, namely sexual interaction and the diverse ways in which people have sex, is quietly pushed to the side in favour of safer topics like sexual anatomy, puberty, menstruation, body hair, hygiene, and pregnancy. If dealt with at all, topics such as the ways of having sexual intercourse, anal intercourse, oral sex, sexual interaction in homosexuality, or group sex are quickly skimmed over. Further, despite these "efforts" it is plain that many parents still see sex as shameful, embarrassing, or bad in some sense and so avoid discussing it with their children. One study, for example, found that more than 40% of children had sexual intercourse before their parents had discussed sex with them.[1]

And this is understandable when authorative providers of sexual information behave in essentially the same way. Thus the Mayo Clinic, a leading US medical centre one would expect to have an enlightened view on giving sexual information, both avoids and recommends avoiding talking openly about sex to children. On its sexual health website it recommends that if a school-age child asks about how people have sex, the parent could simply reply, "The man puts his penis inside the woman's vagina." Not that the woman could also take the man's penis in her mouth or anus, that the man could put his tongue in the woman's vagina, that the man could rub his penis between the woman's breasts, or that they could masturbate each other. Further, if the child asks if two boys or two girls can also have sex, we are told the parent could give the answer—or rather non-answer pretending to be an answer—"Yes, there are many types of intimate relationships including those between two people of the same sex." We are then counselled that, "In this and other issues regarding sexuality, brief answers to specific questions will serve your child best."[2]

But how will it serve the child best to say that sex is when the man puts his penis in the woman's vagina—which effectively means that same-sex people cannot have sex—and then go on to say that two boys or two girls can have sex but not say how? Such brief and contradictory answers can only serve to confuse the child, or at least make her wonder why her parent is confused. For if sex is just the man putting his penis in the woman's vagina, then even a child will understand that two boys or two girls cannot have sex. So why is the parent now saying they can but not offering any explanation of how? The likely answer is that the parent, and the sex educator recommending this approach, wants to make it look like he or she is progressive and open-minded in talking about sex, but at the same time still feels there is something bad about sex and so avoids saying more than the minimum.

TOO MUCH SEX

The same approach is discernible, I feel, in the writings of those scholars who try to argue that there is such a thing as "too much" sex. Such scholars do not typically argue that sex in itself should be avoided, but rather content themselves with arguing that a certain frequency of sex should be avoided. The study I want to look at here, which argues just this and claims to have discovered what counts as excessive levels, is by Niklas Långström and R. Karl Hanson and is entitled "High Rates of Sexual Behaviour in the General Population: Correlates and Predictors."

Although the title implies that the paper will simply be dealing with "high rates" of sexual behaviour, and merely be giving "correlates and predictors" of this behaviour, the claims made in the paper are much more than this. For we are told that it is possible to identify a level of sexual activity that could be considered "excessive." We are even told that this level of excessive sexual activity constitutes a "distinct disorder (hypersexuality)."[3]

Such claims are strangely reminiscent of those made by the mediaeval Christian thinker Augustine (and numerous other moral and religious fundamentalists), who also claimed to have identified excessive rates of sexual behaviour, namely sexual behaviour engaged in "beyond the necessity of procreation."[4] Augustine's criterion is different from Långström and Hanson's, for while Augustine thinks it is non-procreative sex that is excessive, Långström and Hanson think it is a particular frequency of sex that is excessive (any rate of sexual behaviour over the 90th percentile of their sample). Still, both are in agreement in that they think there is such a thing as "excessive" sexual behaviour.

Långström and Hanson, of course, qualify their claims by saying that it is only high rates of "impersonal sex" that can be defined as excessive, not high rates of "personal sex." The difference between these two, we are told, is that impersonal sex is primarily focused on the sex act while personal sex focuses on the person. As examples of impersonal sex they list things like masturbation, pornography use, casual sex, multiple partners, and group sex. Personal sex, however, is "intercourse within romantic relationships." The reason given for this distinction is that while the correlates associated with high rates of impersonal sex are undesirable features (for example, negative physical health and dissatisfaction with psychological health and life in general), those associated with personal sex are not. Indeed, high rates of personal sex are associated with desirable features (for example, high satisfaction with sex life and life in general).

The implication here is that excessive rates of sexual behaviour can lead to bad physical and psychological health. And again, just as Långström and Hanson are in agreement with a mediaeval thinker about the idea that there is such a thing as excessive levels of sexual behaviour, so they are in agreement with other early thinkers about the deleterious physical and psychological effects of such excessive behaviour. In the 15th century sex manual *The Mirror of Coitus*, for example, the author warns us that

> excessive coitus consumes the natural body heat and ignites injurious heat. It also weakens all the bodily members and the natural internal operations. Thus, disequilibrium follows, and for this reason the person becomes debilitated and depressed; his bodily movements are weighed down, and his stomach and liver are weakened; he is unable to digest food, his blood becomes corrupt and he begins to sweat. Excessive coitus causes the principal members to weaken and makes the body grow old long before its time.[5]

Långström and Hanson are not as specific as the author of *The Mirror of Coitus*, but it is quite clear that they are at least in agreement about excessive forms of sexual behaviour leading to negative physical health and dissatisfaction with psychological health and life in general.

Nevertheless, it seems evident that if anyone wants to label a behaviour's rate as "excessive" or as a "distinct disorder," then one should be able to demonstrate that the behavioural rate leads to undesirable physical or psychological consequences. For it makes little clinical sense to label a behaviour rate excessive if nothing about the behaviour rate has been shown to cause any adverse effects. Thus, for example, a certain rate of alcohol consumption is excessive because it has been shown to have the undesirable consequences of alcohol poisoning, sclerosis of the liver, delirium tremens, and other psychological and physical health problems. But just as the author of *The Mirror of Coitus* has nowhere shown that "excessive coitus" "makes the body grow old long before its time," so have Långström and Hanson nowhere shown that the high rates of sexual behaviour they describe cause any undesirable features. All they have shown is that high rates of "impersonal sex" are, in some instances, *correlated* with such features.

However, as Långström and Hanson are aware, correlation does not show causation. And the fact that equally high rates of sexual behaviour in another context, namely romantic relationships, do not lead to such consequences makes it unlikely that it is the high rates of sexual behaviour themselves that cause the undesirable consequences in the "impersonal" context. Indeed, some of the undesirable correlates listed are plainly not consequences of high rates of impersonal sex. Thus, we are told, "In comparison [with high rates of personal sex], the correlates of high rates of impersonal sex were undesirable (or neutral). For both men and women, high rates of impersonal sex were associated with adverse family backgrounds, negative health indicators, and dissatisfaction with life in general."[6]

Obviously, however, an adverse family background is not the consequence of high rates of impersonal sex, for the family background comes before the high rates of impersonal sex, and consequences do not come before their causes. Likewise, it is implausible that negative health is a consequence of purely high rates of impersonal sex. It seems doubtful that masturbation and pornography use (even in high rates) are bad for one's health, though the history of sexology—and religion—is choc-a-bloc with people who at one time believed such things.

One could try to argue, I suppose, that casual sex and multiple partners can have negative health consequences through the greater possibility of catching a sexually transmitted disease. But this is plainly not an inherent consequence of such sexual behaviour. It is rather a consequence of such behaviour *in conjunction with* failing to practise safe sex. Once safe sex is practised, there is little reason why sex with multiple partners needs result in a sexually transmitted disease.

In the same way it seems improbable that high rates of impersonal sex are the cause of dissatisfaction with life in general. This is suggested by Långström and Hanson's own findings. They report that "hypersexuality [i.e. high rates of impersonal sex] in women, in contrast to men, was neither associated with a lower satisfaction with sexual life nor with physical health."[7] And here it seems significant to note that not even negative physical health is related to impersonal sex. But if high rates of impersonal sex are not associated with a woman's level of satisfaction with her sex life, then her high rates of impersonal sex cannot be the cause of her satisfaction or dissatisfaction with her sex life. In other words, a woman with high rates of impersonal sex can well be satisfied with her sex life.[8] And if a woman can be thus satisfied with her sex life, it is hard to believe that such a sex life could be the cause of her dissatisfaction with life in general. To believe this is to hold the implausible view that a satisfying sex life can be the cause of a dissatisfying life.

Of course, the lack of association here was only observed for women. But even with men Långström and Hanson have given us no reason to believe that it is the high rates of impersonal sex that cause dissatisfaction with life in general. The causal relation could easily be the other way around or, more likely, there may be a third factor that is a common cause for both of these variables. High rates of impersonal sex for women and high rates of personal sex for both men and women in a romantic relationship do not lead to dissatisfaction with life in general. This strongly suggests that, in the case of men and impersonal sex, high rates of the sexual behaviour likewise play little causal role in such dissatisfaction.

LÅNGSTRÖM AND HANSON'S REPLY

Långström and Hanson have replied to this criticism by saying, "Giles seems to assume a level of integration of different areas of satisfaction that is not supported by other findings from empirical psychology. Even if a certain area of functioning is non-problematic in itself, it could still lead to unhappiness with life in general." They then give the example of an academic who is very satisfied with his research, spending 60 hours a week in his office. This, however, could then easily lead to problems with his relationships to friends and family. In this sort of case, they conclude, "general satisfaction with life could decrease despite high satisfaction with one's work".[9]

But this is analogy does not fit the point under discussion. For even though it looks like it explains how high rates of impersonal sex for men might lead to a general dissatisfaction with life—these sorts of rates lead men to spend too much time on sex and thus neglect other aspects of their lives—the analogy fails when applied not only to women but also to both men and women in romantic relationships. For both women with high rates of impersonal sex and men and women in romantic relationships with high rates of personal sex show no such general life dissatisfaction.

But why should this analogy be applicable in the one case if it is not applicable in the other two? We are never told. If this analogy were relevant to the point under discussion, it should be the case that while a general dissatisfaction with life might be the result for a man who spends 60 hours a week on his research, such dissatisfaction does not occur for a woman who similarly spends 60 hours a week on her research. But there is no apparent reason why this should be true. A woman in this case should just as easily develop problems with her relationships to friends and family.

Further, if the analogy is to work, then just as there is a distinction between impersonal sex and personal sex, there should be some equivalent distinction between types of time spent at one's office, where high amounts of the "impersonal" time spent at one's office lead men to a general dissatisfaction with life, but high amounts of the "personal" time spent at one's office have no such effect on men or women. But there is no such distinction. According to the analogy, what leads to the general dissatisfaction with life is simply that the man spends high amounts of time at his office. Consequently, this analogy cannot account for the distinction between the different cases and thus fails to support Långström and Hanson's claim that high levels of impersonal sex lead to a general dissatisfaction with life.

Långström and Hanson end their response by saying, "It would be truly amazing if sexuality was the one area of life where restraint was never of benefit."[10] But this remark also misses the point. First, the fact that a behaviour is engaged in at levels that are higher than average does not thereby show that there is no restraint. It might only indicate that the person employs less restraint than other people. Or it might simply show that the person engaged in these behaviours has a higher level of interest in or enjoyment of the behaviour than the average person does.

Putting it in terms of "restraint" makes it sound like the person with lower levels of sexual behaviour is holding herself back and demonstrating self-control while the person with higher levels has given in to her urges and is out of control. This carries with it the idea that the person with lower levels of sexual behaviour is displaying a "moral fortitude," "character strength," or some such laudable quality, by not giving in to a destructive temptation. This in turn suggests that the person with higher levels has some sort of "moral weakness" or "character defect" and therefore cannot resist the temptation. To use the idea of a lack of "restraint" is thus to use biased language that already carries with it the idea that high levels of sexual behaviour are a "disorder." And once again the parallels with religious morality are plain.

But the more likely account is simply that the person with lower levels of sexual behaviour loses interest in or enjoyment of sex more quickly and easily than does the person with higher levels of sexual behaviour. Or, to put it another way, that the person with lower levels of sexual behaviour has less sexual desire than does the person with higher levels.

This view is supported by findings in neurophysiology. In a recent study 39 men and 13 women who fit the profile for hypersexuality, had their brain responses measured while viewing erotic images.[11] What the researchers especially looked at was the brain-wave response during the 300 milliseconds immediately after the image was shown. In people with addictions or compulsive behaviour a sharp spike is shown in the brain wave immediately after viewing something of high interest. This is known as the P300 response and is a neurophysiological way of indicating an addiction or compulsion. The researchers expected that the subjects would similarly show the P300 response, and thus reveal a "sexual addiction" or "sexual compulsion." The results, however, were that none of the subjects demonstrated the P300 response.

This strongly suggests that there is no real relation between hypersexual behaviour and addiction or compulsion. According to Nicole Praust, one of the study's investigators, "The brain's response to sexual pictures was not predicted by any of the three questionnaire measures of hypersexuality.... Brain response was only related to the measure of sexual desire. In other words, hypersexuality does not appear to explain brain responses to sexual images any more than just having a high libido."[12]

Secondly, Långström and Hanson's own data show the inappropriateness of their remark about the benefits of restraint. For if it is of benefit to restrain one's levels of sexual behaviour, then it should be of benefit for both women engaging in impersonal sex and men and women engaging in personal sex in a romantic relationship also to restrain their sexual behaviour. But Långström and Hanson's own data show that in both these situations high levels of sexual behaviour have no adverse correlates. Consequently, it is unclear what sort of benefits they could reap from "restraining" their behaviour.

With this it should be clear that Långström and Hanson have not produced any evidence or arguments for the view that there is such a thing as "excessive" levels of sexual behaviour or a "distinct disorder" of hypersexuality. Rather, it seems that, like the claims of Augustine, their assertions here are merely attempts to stigmatize a type of sexual behaviour of which they morally disapprove.

7
Age Dysphoria

A Case Study

WHAT IS AGE DYSPHORIA?

In this essay I want to explore an atypical condition in which sexual desire plays an important role in order to see how sexual desire is related to the condition. The condition I have in mind has been variously called "sexual infantilism,"[1] "autonepiophilia" or "paraphilic infantilism,"[2] and "adult baby syndrome."[3] It consists of an adult who identifies with being an infant or child and feels a compulsion to act and dress like one. Further, these individuals lack an interest in adult-like sexual activity and are instead sexually aroused by the idea of being an infant or child and what it implies.[4] The sexual component seems often central to this condition with sexual desire, fantasies, masturbation, and sexual interactions being frequently based upon or centred on the idea of being a baby or child.

Persons with this condition appear more or less continuously to feel this compulsion to act like an infant or child. They do not, however, continually act on it, but rather typically reserve times to do so when they are alone, with others with the same condition, or with someone accepting of their condition.

Further, although there appears to be both males and females with this condition, the overwhelming majority seem to be males. For example, Thomas John Speaker was able to recruit 12 males but only one female for his study, while in their large online study Kaitlyn Hawkinson and Brian D. Zamboni were able to recruit 1, 795 males and only 139 females.[5]

The age of the child that the adult identifies with can vary. Although some people here identify with being an infant or very young child, others can identify with being a pre-pubescent child.[6] Because of these variations, terms that include words like "infantilism" or "baby" can be misleading. Further, since this condition seems driven by a sense of being constantly unhappy with being an adult,[7] referring to the condition as "age dysphoria" seems appropriate, where the term "dysphoria" is understood (as in gender dysphoria) to refer to an intense unhappiness. This is not to suggest a new diagnostic category, but only a term that is less misleading.

Sometimes one of the persons will take the role of what they call a "mummy" or "daddy" while the other will play the role of the baby or child. Items of clothing here that often are of major importance are nappies or diapers and rubber pants. But other things like cribs, baby bottles, pacifiers, and baby toys can also be brought in. These sessions also frequently involve sexual fantasies and masturbation and often sexual interaction with the person playing the parental role. This sexual interaction can be blended with the role playing. Thus, one man reports that as his "mummy" was changing his diaper, she stopped and performed fellatio him for a while before finishing changing him. He then pulled his diaper partially down and had sexual intercourse with her.[8]

Because of this erotic aspect of the condition, it is easy to confuse it with similar erotic but apparently distinct conditions. These are fetishism tied to baby clothes—especially diapers and rubber pants—or the related "transvestic" condition of being sexually aroused by dressing like a baby or child. Although there is little research on such conditions, Caldwell suggests that they are different from what I am calling age dysphoria and primarily involve elements of paraphilia, impulsive dyscontrol, or obsessive compulsivity.[9] Such conditions do not seem mainly based on the experience of age dysphoria and the idea of identifying with being a child. Caldwell, for example, gives a case study of an individual with a fetishistic-transvestic relation to diapers. This subject is sexually aroused by diapers and focuses his sexual awareness solely on them, wearing them and masturbating with them. He does not fantasize about being a baby, nor does he show any desires to be a baby or deep unhappiness about being an adult. In other words, he has no dysphoria over his age. Speaker also gives examples of such individuals. Nevertheless, it is plain that persons with age dysphoria and those with such fetishism-transvestism show similar behaviours. These are sexual behaviours involving babies' or children's clothing. The question, however, of just how the sexual desires and behaviour in age dysphoria are related to the identification with being a child is unclear.

In an attempt to show the relation between these elements, to criticize other accounts, and to get a fuller understanding of this condition, I shall now present a case of a person with age dysphoria.

CASE

The subject is a 45-year-old white Canadian male who contacted me after reading an article of mine. He identifies with being an infant and was happy to see my use of the term "age dysphoria," as he felt it captured a central and underlying feature of his condition. He first contacted me under a pseudonym, but after an agreement of confidentiality he used his real name. He is university-educated and has read much of the academic literature on his condition. He expressed concern that the condition was not properly understood and wanted to explain his condition to me, hoping that I could explore the condition further. After hearing his account I suggested the idea of doing a case study. He was keen on this, but also wanted to maintain anonymity. He then sent me a detailed account of the development and experience of his condition.

The account was well-written and thoughtful, showing a fair amount of insight. We had several e-mail exchanges wherein I asked him specific questions about his condition. I then had two semi-structured interviews with him using internet video conferencing. I also had him sign an informed consent document. I will first present his written account. This will be followed by a discussion where I bring in further details from both our correspondence and the interviews. To help maintain the subject's privacy, various identifying factors have been removed or changed. I have also edited his account for length, removing material that was not directly relevant to his condition. Here is his written account:

> I was born into a very dysfunctional family consisting of my mother, who was a severe alcoholic with underlying mental health issues, and my sister, who is three years older. My father was completely absent until I was 12. Besides drinking daily, my mother experienced some psychotic breaks, where she believed that a complex network of Mafia and bikers were chasing our small family to torment us for some reason. She was very physically abusive to us. For example, when I was five, she threw a padlock at me, splitting my head open. Another time, she beat me senseless with a fishing rod, whipping me all over my body in a rage. I use these examples to illustrate that she had little concern for the consequences of her actions when she was angry, but there were many more. She was very neglectful as well, and would leave us on the steps of a pub while she drank inside. Food was scarce; my older sister would sometimes steal money from her purse to buy us a bag of chips.
>
> The abuse was compounded by her constant relocating. Since she felt she was being chased, we moved from town to town every few months, with very little financial support to do so. At times, we were living in abandoned houses, or even abandoned cars. I was in and out of at least 17 primary schools by the time I was 11. She taught us very early not to talk to authorities, and managed to keep a low enough profile, so child services were not involved. Most of what I remember, however, is being alone, because she would obsess about her

situation with my sister for hours each day, and I would go out wandering in the town we happened to be in at that time. My mother seemed at best unconcerned for me, at worst disgusted with me. Her own family of origin was much worse, she described horrific physical, emotional, and sexual abuse on a daily basis, and she made it clear to me that men were awful.

These are the worst parts, but there were moments of stability and hope. I distinctly remember a few Christmas holidays that had all the regular decorations, toys, and I even remember having my own room decorated with snoopy curtains and Star Wars bed sheets for a period of time when I was perhaps eight or nine. My mother was a very passionate and warm mother at times and very strong and wonderful soul when she was sober and healthy. A lot of my memories before the age of 11 are patchy, fuzzy, and jumbled, but I felt loved by her at times, and I felt lucky to have her as a mother.

So in this context my adult baby interests developed. I remember being in the hospital for asthma at perhaps the age of three, and I was forced into diapers by a couple of nurses while I was kicking and screaming, because I was having accidents. My actual interest in babyish things began later, perhaps at the age of four or five. I have this clear memory of my sister and I looking after a younger baby, who was two, while our two mothers went out drinking. At some point, my sister and I were playing house, and she wanted to dress me up as a baby. I put on one of the younger boy's diapers, and some of his clothes, and was in heaven. I was obsessed with the idea of wetting and messing the diaper, and though my sister got bored and moved on to playing something else, I was squatting in different corners of the house, trying to go to the toilet in my diaper.

After this point, I mostly kept my desires to myself, but I was at times fascinated with having accidents and fantasizing that I was being turned into a baby. I didn't actually have many accidents, though I did go through a short bed-wetting stint when I was perhaps seven. Some adult babies report that they would sneak diapers or baby clothes and dress up in private when they were children, but I did not engage in this part until I hit puberty.

At the age of 12 my father appeared in my life and decided to raise me from that point. I was taken out of my mother's care and placed with him and his wife in a different city. His life was better. He was a mechanic, a regular working guy, but he was a daily alcoholic, and he seldom talked to me or played with me, so the pattern of being alone continued. At 12 I was already in the strange mind set of being grateful for having a child's body, while wishing I was much younger. As I began to masturbate, I would think of myself as a toddler or baby while doing so, and the acting out in private began. I wet my pants in the car one day, but was not discovered. I took those urine-soaked jeans and hid them in my closet. At night I would take them out, put them on and fantasize that I was a toddler and had wet myself. I would masturbate while having these fantasies.

By 14 I had stolen a diaper from my grandmother's closet (she kept a few diapers around for her younger grandchildren) and was masturbating with it. I wanted so badly to be taken care of, to let go of all my responsibilities and be babied. Things began to fall apart with my dad's life . . . he divorced his wife and moved across the country to live with his mother, and was drinking heavily. I was chronically late and failed to meet my responsibilities, and he was very frustrated with me. I spent hours and hours each day in video game arcades, and was smoking cigarettes behind his back. I was not getting along at school, being bullied and teased by other kids for being "different." Things reached a crisis point when I threw a chair across the classroom in frustration one day, and the school started testing me with a psychologist. I suppose they deduced that I was well above average intelligence, and I was put in another school, where I did not get along, but where the bullying was milder.

My father's frustration with me came to a head, and one night he kicked me out, at 14. Rather than try to repair the situation, I looked up my mother, and managed to get back to the city she was living in. Of course, things had got much worse for her and my sister by this point, and I left to live on the street at 15.

I lived on and off the streets for the next five years, doing LSD and pot, hanging out in arcades, and living in homeless shelters, mostly alone, or having one other street buddy that I hung around with. I had a religious experience at 17, and worked in a religious homeless shelter for a year. One of my tasks was to look after the shelter alone for the graveyard shift, and that was when I would dress up in diapers and women's clothes from the clothing room.

By this point, I had discovered adult diapers, and I was always sneaking off and wearing them while masturbating. I did not develop sexually at all. I went through the motions, and acted like I was interested in women, but I wasn't interested in either sex—I only wanted to be a baby. I would lie in my bed at night and pray to be turned into a baby.

At 20 I decided to make a big effort to get off the street. I got a job, and met a girlfriend, who became my first wife. Sex with her was spotty at best, I found I could orgasm inside her if I fantasized that I was shrinking at the exact right moment, but otherwise, I was impotent. We managed to rent an apartment, and she looked after the bills and organizing while I went to work each day. We did a lot of pot and LSD, though, and the relationship came to an end four years later. I entered a one-month addiction treatment program at the age of 25, and started to process my childhood pain in daily group therapy sessions. These sessions saved my life and my mind; I would never again return to the street. I discovered that there was a whole world of healthy good things beyond the small dysfunctional world I had been living in. I remained drug free and went back to school.

My adult baby thing had progressed and deepened. I was going out into parks late at night, wanting to be seen by others, but terrified to be caught. I would go into a bush, change into a diaper, and challenge myself to walk down a short pathway in nothing but a diaper and t-shirt. There has always been an exhibitionist streak in me, but I was seldom seen by anybody. I used to go to a park that was frequented by gay men in the middle of the night, and I did manage to approach a few of them once or twice, talking to them about my desires. They lost interest when they discovered I wasn't gay, however.

I met my second wife when I was 31. It was the same thing as the first marriage—she handled the finances, the organizing, and I handled the ideas and set the pace. She then became pregnant and settled down to raise our new daughter.

This second marriage lasted longer, my wife gave birth to our second daughter few years after, and I continued to go to work each day. Of course, our sex life was unacceptable to her. She was not interested in babying me, though she tried it a few times, and I was not interested in much other than playing video games, art, music, and wearing diapers. I had a social life of sorts while I was with her, but mostly it was for her—I don't get along with adults very well, it seems.

When my wife left me at the age of 41, I continued with my work. What was this strange thing that I could never put down and why wasn't I like anybody else? At 41 I had never even managed to own a car, let alone think about buying a house. I still rode a skateboard to work, or a bicycle. I had no interest in typical adult behaviours like cocktail parties, golf, or financial investments. I went online to get more involved in the "ABDL" [adult baby/diaper lover] community, and started to acquire more babyish things. I built a crib, collected baby toys and adult-sized baby clothes, and started to embrace the more nurturing side of ABDL. I have had experiences that are nothing short of incredible in my crib, listening to adult baby visualization audio files, and sucking on a bottle, or my thumb. I dropped many of my friends for various reasons—though maintaining my relationship to my kids, who I see regularly. I am now exploring relationships with other people who have similar ABDL interests.

DISCUSSION

This report gives a detailed account of the early beginnings of a case of age dysphoria, showing how fantasies about being a baby appeared, became eroticized, and persisted into adulthood, becoming the focus of the subject's life. As a young child he fantasized about being turned into a baby. His eroticizing of these fantasies in a clearly genitally-centred way started with his masturbation, which, he told me, appeared, shortly after he turned 12. It seems significant, however, that something resembling erotic fantasizing was already present at an early age. He says, for example, that when he was first dressed as a baby by his sister at the age of four or five he was "in heaven." Although it is unclear, this might well be his way of describing the sensual feeling he had when the baby clothes transported him for the first time back into the world of being a baby. If this is so, then it might well be that an erotic element in his condition was there from the very start. For this memory seems to be of the beginnings of his condition.

One can always be sceptical over the veracity of memories reaching back to when the person was four or five, but research shows that people are quite capable of having accurate autobiographical memories by the ages of four and five, with the majority of people's first memories going back to three or three-and-a-half years of age.[10] Indeed, several researchers have been able to collect alleged first memories that go back to before the age of two. In about half of these cases the parents of the subjects were able to confirm the accuracy of the memories.[11] This suggests that the subject's memory of his sister dressing him as a baby and his experiencing it as heaven might well be true.

Again, there are aspects of his condition that look like fetishism for baby clothes, but it seems clear that what held his real interest was the idea of being a baby, not merely baby clothes themselves, though of course the clothes helped him pursue his real interest. Thus, when he wet himself in his jeans, he later used these jeans to masturbate, even though they were not baby clothes. For the fantasies accompanying his masturbation were about being a toddler who had wet himself. Further, if this was simply a fetish about urine-soaked clothing, then the fantasy of himself being a toddler would probably not come into it. In clothing fetishes the article of clothing seems to take on its power by symbolizing the body or body part of the other person, perhaps becoming something of an inanimate extension of the body.[12]

It is evident that the erotic pleasure resulting from his repeated masturbation would have served to reinforce and strengthen his ties to his fantasies. I do not feel, however, that such masturbation plays a crucial role in the development of his age dysphoria. For the erotic pleasure, albeit in a child-like form, was already there in the fantasies from an earlier age.

Further, as I have argued elsewhere, erotic pleasure is not the goal of sexual desire, but rather a confirmation that the activity that leads to the pleasure is the desired activity. When someone engages in a sexual act or fantasizes about such an act, the erotic pleasure arises as a way of saying, "Yes! This is what you really desire!" And this remains true even if the person, for other reasons, would choose not to act on the desire or ever expect to fulfil it. I have argued these points at length in *The Nature of Sexual Desire* and so will not repeat my arguments here. In the case of the subject of this study, what he really desires is to be a baby. Thus, he says, "I would lie in my bed at night and pray to be turned into a baby" (I will address the question of the strength of this feeling shortly). Whenever he fantasized about being a baby, erotic pleasure would be the response. Therefore, when he began to masturbate it was natural that it would be done to the fantasies that already gave him erotic pleasure.

But how is it that fantasizing about being a baby can give rise to erotic pleasure? Since erotic pleasure is the confirmation of sexual desire, then sexual desire should be present in the fantasy about being a baby. But how, exactly is his sexual desire connected to the idea of being a baby? The answer is given, I would argue, in seeing that it is not simply the idea of being a baby that is the object of sexual desire. Rather, it is what being a baby implies. This is suggested by looking to the earliest experiences of his condition. For here it was not just that he was playing at being a baby, but rather was playing at being a baby for his sister or, rather, for a female who played a motherly role towards him.

In this play session it seems not unlikely that his sister was touching and, no doubt, intimately stimulating his naked skin while getting him to take off his clothes and helping put diapers and baby clothes on him. Because of this, I would argue, his erotic fantasies of being a baby are intimately tied to the fantasy of being cared for and caressed like a baby. This is why, it would seem, it is erotically pleasurable for him to fantasize about being a baby, namely, because it implies being treated like a baby by a female caressing him and showing him motherly care.

This fits with my point made in Essay 3, namely, that the decisive object of sexual desire is the mutual baring and caressing of bodies. In fact the taking off of his clothes is just the baring of his body to her bare hands, hands that probably helped to dress him while touching and stroking him. In being thus caressed, his naked skin would also caress the skin of her hands.

But then he says that she got bored and moved on to playing other things. He, however, continued playing at being a baby, squatting and trying to go to soil his diaper. But why should he continue to do this? One likely answer is that he was aware that diapers that are soiled have to be changed. Consequently, if he could soil his diaper, then his sister might well come back and, showing him motherly care, change him—that is, bare and caress him again. Here it is evident how baring and caressing, which are the object of sexual desire, became, for him, intimately connected to the idea of being treated like a baby by a mother figure.

In *Sexual Attraction: The Psychology of Allure* I argue that the experience of sexual attraction not only involves attraction to the other person, but also the fantasized image of oneself in an intimate physical union with the attractive person. To give an account of the subject's age dysphoria in terms of sexual attraction, then, one could say that what he is sexually attracted to is the idea of his body as a baby intimately brought together with the body of a woman who treats him in a baby-like way.[13]

The same idea is expressed by a subject in Speaker's study:—"I feel a tremendous release in diapers, like I am loved and cared for."[14] Here dressing like a baby strongly implies being loved and cared for like a baby by a "mummy." A natural question to ask here is whether being "loved and cared for" like a baby has anything to do with eroticism. Yet this very subject reports that he masturbates every time he wears diapers. So clearly from his own perspective the idea of being loved and cared for like a baby is an erotic experience. However, although he is married to a woman who is his regular sex partner, he has not attempted to involve her in his infant-like erotic activities, which he keeps secret from her. The reason for his secrecy seems to be that he has anxiety over the idea of his wife learning about his sexuality and guilt over his "baby desires." Thus, it is not that he has no interest in her being involved in his sexual activities, it is rather that he dare not involve her because of fear and guilt.

It could, of course, be doubted that my subject really wanted, in any deep sense, to be a baby. After all, he did have work and other things that would be impossible for a baby to have. Were these not important to him? And if they were, should he not be aware that being a real baby would imply the loss of them? By way of answer to this question I can relate a conversation he told me about that he had with a male-to-female transsexual. The transsexual said to him that "The difference between you and me is that I continually feel like a woman, whereas you only feel like a baby some of the time. Those are the times when you dress and act like a baby."

He strongly objected to this, replying that he did feel like a baby all the time and desperately wanted to be one, just like a transsexual desperately wants to be the opposite sex. The real difference, he said, was that while the transsexual was able to act continually like a woman, and indeed could survive by doing so, he was not able to act continually like a baby, at least not if he wanted to survive. His deeply held feeling of being a baby "trapped inside an adult body" was, he said, just as constant and real as the transsexual's deeply held feeling of being a woman "trapped inside a man's body."

This is an interesting point. For although a male-to-female transsexual might be able to "pass" as a real woman, and live out her life acting like a woman, an "adult-to-baby transageist," as one could call him to underline this point, cannot. There is no operation or hormones that will enable him or her to resemble a baby. But this does not mean that the person with age dysphoria is any less dysphoric than someone with gender dysphoria. Nor does it imply that of his or her sense of identifying with a baby is any less driven or powerful that a transsexual's sense of identifying with the opposite sex. It simply means he or she does not have the same options available as the gender dysphoric person has and so must adjust his life accordingly. For while a male-to-female transsexual can (at least in some cultures) go out and get a job while dressing and acting like a woman, the age dysphoric person cannot go out and get a job while dressing and acting like a baby.

Consequently, the person with age dysphoria must simply put his or her sense of identity and dysphoria to one side and, for most of the time, behave like an adult. Here it should be mentioned that one of the things the subject did in an attempt to make himself achieve a continuous baby-like state was to regularly shave off all his body hair.

As just mentioned, it is crucial to note that the condition I am describing is not one where the idea of being a baby itself has become eroticized. Such a condition is described by Freund and Blanchard, who refer to a small group of paedophiles who, they claim, "are sexually aroused by the thought of being children themselves."[15] According to Freund and Blanchard such persons have what they call an "erotic target location error." That is, their erotic target—which is children—has been erroneously located to be their own bodies. This is the same mechanism, they say, that occurs in cases of heterosexual male-to-female transsexualism, or autogynephilia, something I discussed in the first essay. Here, the transsexual's erotic target—which is women—has been erroneously located to his own body. The autogynephile is therefore sexually aroused by the idea of being a woman.

It should be clear, however, that being sexually aroused by the thought of being a child—which might be termed "autopaedophilia"[16]—is different from the eroticism I have been discussing. For nothing about the subject in this case study indicates his real erotic target is children, or that he has erroneously located this target to his own body. On the contrary, it is quite clear, as I shall demonstrate shortly, that he is sexually aroused by adult women. Further, I cannot see that any of the subjects in Speaker's study have a autopaedophilic orientation. One of the subjects says he is fascinated by small children and likes interacting with them. But this is simply because he likes to imagine being a small child himself. The common age-dysphoric desire for a "mummy" or "daddy," which seems to be absent in autopaedophilia, suggests age dysphoria has little to do with paedophilia or even autopaedophilia.[17] This is not to deny the drivenness of the age-dysphoric desires, it is merely to give a fuller account of the desires.

With my subject it is easy to miss the point that desiring to be a baby implies being caressed like a baby, because he says various things that seem to go against it. He says, for example, "I went through the motions, and acted like I was interested in women, but I wasn't interested in either sex—I only wanted to be a baby." Other things he says, however, suggest that it is being treated like a baby by another person that plays an important role in his desire. For example, he says of his first wife that he found he could orgasm inside her if he fantasized he was shrinking at exactly the right moment. That is, he could have sex with her and even have orgasms if he imagined he was becoming small like a baby. In other words, he was able to attain erotic pleasure during sex if he imagined himself as a baby having sex with an adult female.

He also says of his second wife that his sexual desires were unacceptable to her because she had no interest in babying him. Therefore, I would argue, it is not that he is sexually uninterested in women. Rather, it is that he is uninterested in sex where he has to comport himself as an adult having adult-like sex with a woman. He further says at the end of his account that he is "now exploring relationships with other people who have similar ABDL interests," which also betrays a sexual interest in other people.

What he sexually desires, then, is sex with a woman who treats him like a baby. So praying to be turned into a baby should be understood to mean "praying to be turned into a baby *so that I can be erotically caressed as a baby by a motherly figure*." This is also suggested by what he told me in the interviews. In the first interview he mentioned that he was in a sexual relationship with another age-dysphoric person who was also a male-to-female transsexual. Both the subject and his sexual partner identified with being infants and therefore both wanted to be babied by each other. That is, they both wanted each other to be the parent. He wanted his partner to be the "mummy" and his partner wanted him to be the "daddy." They dealt with this problem, as many age-dysphoric sex partners do, by taking turns playing the parent. A major problem for an individual with age dysphoria, the subject told me, is to find a partner who is happy to play the parental role. Because of this, people with age dysphoria typically resort to taking turns.

In the second interview he told me this relationship had ended and that he was now in a relationship with a non-age-dysphoric biological woman. He had known this woman for several years as an acquaintance, and even let her know once, during a truth or dare game at a party, that he was an "adult baby", whereupon she replied jokingly, "I'd wipe your bottom!" Several years later they became romantically interested in each other, went out for dinner, and sat on the beach afterwards talking about relationships. He reminded her of his age dysphoria, saying, "I may never be able to give you what you need sexually, because I am not a sexual person in the same way." She agreed to give the "baby thing" a try. Much to their surprise, the results were remarkable. Thus, he told me,

> She is not only interested in every single aspect of my little lifestyle; she is incredibly turned on by it. That is everything from feeding to diaper changes to bathing and nursing. To illustrate: she once was playing peek-a-boo with me while I was nursing, and she had an orgasm spontaneously (impossible to fake for her because she is a squirter, she and expels a huge amount of fluid when she cums) because she was so turned on by how "little" I was acting.

He then said,

> We now experience a growing sex life that gets deeper each time. She has a recurring fantasy that I am shrinking and entering her womb and it makes her orgasm over and over during sex. I am often in a puddle of her fluid at the end. We also have wonderful cuddling sessions that can last for hours. I am very much in love with this woman.

It is noteworthy how his new partner's fantasy complements his own earlier fantasy with his first wife of shrinking while having sex. During the extended cuddling sessions, he says, he always has an erection. His having found a partner with a sexual interest in playing the mummy role has led to the subject having an active sex life based on sexual intercourse. In my last contact with him he said,

> I am currently having penis–vagina sex with mutual orgasms at least once per day, and often two or three times per day (sometimes as high as five times in

> one day!). Again, a massive and unexpected twist, because I considered myself non-sexual before her.

By "non-sexual" he does not mean lacking in sexual desire or sexual arousal. For his account shows that he engages in masturbation, sexual fantasies, and even sexual interactions with his partners that involve fantasies. All of this points to the existence of sexual desire and sexual arousal. What he seems to mean, then, by "non-sexual" is that he considered himself lacking in sexual desire towards other people, or at least that he had given up on the idea of finding a long-term partner who he could satisfy sexually or who would be able to satisfy him sexually. This is what he meant when he first warned his new partner that "I may never be able to give you what you need sexually, because I am not a sexual person in the same way." However, with an appropriate partner it is clear that he does have sexual desire towards other people.

His real interest in women, however, might be called into question by three things described in his case history. These are his dressing in women's clothes during his graveyard shift, his approaching gay men at night to talk about his desires, and his sexual relationship with a male-to-female transsexual. When I asked him about these, he laughed and said he was aware that it might appear as though he had a sexual interest in men, but assured me that this was not the case. The women's clothes he would put on were night dresses and other "cute" garments that would help him to fantasize he was a baby.

His dressing in diapers, or "baby drag" as he called it, and approaching gay men at night was an attempt to find someone who would accept him as a baby. He was aware that gay men were a sexual minority and thought that they might not see him as being so deviant, and thus be more accepting of his fantasy about being a baby.

As for his transsexual partner, he repeatedly told me how good she was at passing for a biological woman. He himself had no idea she was a transsexual when they first met through an ABDL website. When after several Skype sessions she eventually told him she was a transsexual—which she wanted to do before they met face-to-face—he was shocked but wanted to be open-minded, especially since he wanted people to be open-minded and accepting of himself. Although he decided to give it a go, he was nevertheless concerned that various tell-tale masculine signs, like the person's smell, might put him off, which they eventually did. He also said she had other problems, and lived in another country and would not be able to immigrate to his country.

All of this strongly suggests that the subject's apparent lack of interest in women and only wanting to be a baby is really just a lack of interest in women who would not want to baby him and have sex with him during such "mummy–baby" sessions. This means that his sense of identification with being baby along with the eroticism involved in this identification can only be understood in relation to his desire to be treated like a baby by a "mummy."

But if this is the case, why could he not simply desire to be treated like a baby while continuing to identify with being an adult? One does not, after all, have to act like a baby in order to be babied. The answer, it seems, is that the sort of babying that he finds satisfying, both sexually and emotionally, is the extensive caring that a mother shows towards an infant or young toddler, namely, changing, bathing, feeding, nursing, and "peek-a-boo" games. If one deeply desires these sorts of interactions, then plainly one has to act the role of a baby: one cannot, for example, be fed like a baby unless one feeds like a baby. Further, it seems evident that acting the baby role while receiving such treatment lends a realism to the babying that would not be there otherwise. This realism seems important because it helps the subject feel he has achieved what he really desires, thus helping him to achieve emotional and sexual fulfilment.

With this I hope to have come closer to an understanding of age dysphoria. I have tried to do this by showing how the account of sexual desire as the desire for a mutual baring and caressing of bodies, which applies in more usual forms of sexual desire, can also be applied in and thus help to make sense of a highly atypical case of sexual desire. There are, of course, limitations on what one is able to conclude from a single case study, and it is not my purpose to argue that the findings of this study can be generalized. Whether and to what degree they can be must await further investigation.

8
Naked Love

The Evolution of Human Hairlessness

THE NAKED SKIN OF BARING AND CARESSING

At the end of the third essay I suggested that one of the things that make the biological view of sexual desire attractive is that it emphasizes the essential connection between sexual desire and our physical bodies. I argued, however, that one can easily accept this connection without signing on to the related view that biological processes are the origin of sexual desire. This is because sexual desire is deeply connected to the body simply by the fact that the object of sexual desire is the mutual baring and caressing of bodies. In this final essay I want to explore a crucial feature of this object of desire, namely the nakedness or hairlessness of the bodies that sexual desire aims to bare and caress.

My interest here, however, is in the ultimate rather than proximate causes of naked skin. In Essay 3, it will be recalled, I examined the view that sex hormones are the proximate cause of sexual desire. Here I want to look at the ultimate cause or evolutionary origins of naked skin. In other words, I want to explore how this central feature of our sexual biology made its appearance in the human condition. This exploration should give us insight into how naked skin came to play the major role it does in sexual desire and, as a result, in romantic love.

THEORIES OF HAIRLESSNESS

It has long been a question for evolutionary anthropologists why human beings are nearly completely devoid of body hair. This is a puzzle because all other primates have thick coats of fur or body hair. We too, of course, have body hair. However, human body hair is for the most part extremely fine and short and thus practically invisible. It is this apparent invisibility of human body hair that is normally referred to by the idea of human hairlessness. This peculiar difference from other primates suggests the primate ancestors of human beings likewise had such thick body hair. This is also suggested by the fact that during the third trimester of gestation the human foetus is covered with a fine fur, a fur that disappears prior to birth. Therefore, for some evolutionary reason or reasons, human beings effectively lost their body hair, while nevertheless retaining hair in other places.

Various theories have been put forward to explain this peculiar state of near nakedness. In this essay I want to argue that these accounts are not fully adequate and present a new theory. This theory, which I call the naked love theory, locates the origin of human hairlessness in the mother–infant relationship and what I call maternal selection for hairless infants. The hairlessness that began to appear in this context was then, I will argue, reinforced by sexual selection in the male–female sexual relationship. Although this dual process alone might have produced hairlessness, it could also have been supplemented by other processes that likewise selected for hairlessness.

There are numerous theories of human hairlessness. I will here examine the best known of these. One explanation for hairlessness comes from the aquatic ape theory.[1] According to this account, between 6 and 8 million years ago our ancestors went through a phase in which they were marooned on islands in the Afar triangle area of East Africa. As a result they spent much of their time in aquatic environments. The loss of body hair was an adaptation to this environment. For just as dolphins lost their hair in order to facilitate aquatic locomotion, so did human ancestors.

But this theory fails for various reasons. First, it does not adequately account for why we have maintained this supposedly aquatic feature so long after we left the water. Secondly, even if early human ancestors did spend time in aquatic environments, they never evolved to the point where they could do more than paddle about for short amounts of time. Consequently, they never evolved into anything vaguely resembling the streamlined design of dolphins or other aquatic mammals. It seems unlikely that hairlessness would have helped much. Thirdly, we know that the aquatic environments in these regions were teeming then with crocodiles and other dangerous animals. The non-streamlined, defenceless aquatic ape would not have survived long.

Pagel and Bodmer suggest that human hairlessness evolved in order to free our ancestors from external parasites such as fleas, ticks, and lice.[2] But as they themselves realize, this is challenged by the fact that human beings are still beleaguered with pubic, underarm, and head hair parasites. If the avoidance of external parasites was a good enough reason for shedding most of our body hair, it seems it should have been a good enough reason for shedding all of it. Moreover, since the majority of fur-bearing mammals are also harassed with external parasites, why have they not lost their fur for similar reasons?

Further, even if loss of body hair protects one from fleas, ticks, and lice, it also fully exposes one to attacks from mosquitoes, biting flies, and other such insects. Pagel and Bodmer are seemingly aware of this problem and respond by suggesting that body fur does not offer much defence. But even if it is true that a thick coat of fur does not offer much defence (which is questionable), it is still strides ahead of naked skin that offers absolutely no defence. This theory provides no clear answers to these problems.

A further theory is that human ancestors lost their fur as a way of dealing with overheating. According to a recent version, this overheating occurred because our ancestors moved out into the savannah and started hunting and incorporating meat into their diet. This led to an increase in bodily heating. The evidence for this, we are told, comes from stone tools and butchered animal remains in the fossil record about 2.6 million years ago. According to Jablonski, a proponent of this theory, "Carnivorous animals therefore need to range farther and wider than their herbivorous counterparts to procure a sufficient amount of food … which means predators must expend that much more energy to obtain a meal."[3] This, she says, was just the circumstance in which early human ancestors found themselves.

The major problem with this theory is that stone tools and a few butchered bones are hardly evidence to show that human ancestors were in a situation that resembled that of carnivorous animals. Stone tools can be used for numerous things that have nothing to do with meat eating: defence, making wooden tools, digging for roots, pulverizing tough foods, cracking open nuts, and so on. Both capuchin monkeys and chimpanzees use stone tools for cracking nuts.[4] And although butchered bones might indicate some degree of meat eating, the bones could merely be those of carcasses that were occasionally found and eaten in the absence of other foods.

A more serious point against this theory is that even if it were true that the males were out running and hunting in this way, it is clear that the females could not have been. In these times before birth control females would have been either continually pregnant, nursing infants, or tending to small children. They would not have been expending energy to chase prey across the savannah. As a result, they would not have had any selection pressure to lose their body hair in order to remain cool. Perhaps males could have passed on their hairlessness to females. But if it is male hairlessness that was selected for, why do females have even less body hair than males? If there were to be a difference between male and female hairlessness, it seems it should be the males who would have less hair. But they do not. The fact that females are more hairless than males strongly suggests that it was female hairlessness that was initially selected for. It is unclear how this theory could account for this higher degree of female hairlessness.

Another theory is offered by Harris.[5] In her view, hairlessness was selected for by a parental choice based on cultural standards of beauty. Hairless infants were seen as beautiful and kept whereas hairy infants were seen as ugly and abandoned or killed. This is because they resembled Neanderthals who, Harris argues, had thick coats of fur and were seen as prey by *Homo sapiens*.

Although this theory, I feel, moves in the right direction by seeing parental choice as playing a role, it flounders in several other ways. First, it places the appearance of hairlessness far too late in human evolution.[6] Secondly, it assumes that there was a unified cultural standard of beauty across widely scattered populations of human beings. Thirdly, it depends on the unlikely idea that Neanderthals had fur. Harris thinks they must have had fur because they lived in a cold climate and had not invented the needle, which was essential to make clothes. But awl-like points and knife-like blades have been discovered at Neanderthal sites. Together these could have been used to make holes in animal skins and cut strips of skin to weave through the holes, thus binding skins together to make clothes.[7] Finally, it offers no explanation for why a group of individuals would have hairlessness as a standard of beauty when they themselves were also hair-covered.

A more plausible theory is suggested by Darwin.[8] In his view, hairlessness has no direct advantage and therefore cannot have evolved through natural selection. Rather, he feels, human hairlessness evolved through sexual selection where males came to see the nakedness of the female skin as being sexually attractive. The evidence for this is that human females are everywhere more hairless than males. This in turn, he argues, is evidence that human hairlessness has its evolutionary roots in our female semi-human progenitors. These females must then have transmitted their hairlessness to a near-equal degree to both their female and male offspring. In other words, male hairlessness resulted simply as a genetic correlation with female hairlessness.

This account is important because it recognizes the sexual significance of naked skin, especially naked female skin. However, it still lacks an explanation for why females might have a preference for hairless males and why female hairlessness was selected for in the first place.

The difficulties facing these theories show that human hairlessness has not been fully explained. In attempting to give such an explanation I will now turn to the naked love theory of human hairlessness.

THE ROLE OF BIPEDALISM

It is generally agreed that the prime mover in human evolution was bipedalism. A common view is that bipedalism was an adaptation to the thinning out of the African rainforests. This resulted from a global cooling and subsequent drying that began between 16 and 11 million years ago. Because of this drying out, our early arboreal or semi-arboreal ancestors began to become isolated in patches of forests that were more or less cut off from other wooded areas by open country.[9] This meant that food sources within the trees in the isolated forest groves were quickly used up. There was a pressure on these early pre-hominin ancestors to come down out of the trees and leave their isolated wooded regions in search of other groves and food sources. This state of affairs would probably have favored those individuals who had a tendency to a rudimentary bipedalism.

Crossing the grasslands on two feet rather than on all fours had many benefits. It enabled the individual to stand tall enough to look for the closest woodlands or to spot predators.[10] It also freed the arms to carry food[11] and to gather seeds and nuts.[12]

However, with every beneficial adaptation, there is also a cost. One of the great costs of bipedalism was the loss of prehensile feet and toes. This was due to a selection for shorter toes in relation to the soles of the feet, the arching of the feet, and for a big toe that was more in line with the other toes, thus losing its ability to act like an opposing thumb. All of this rendered the feet unsuitable for grasping.

Although we often think of the objects that an arboreal ape grasps with its feet as being primarily branches, there is also something else that it must be able to grasp with its feet; as an infant, it must be able to grasp the fur of its mother. Both the gibbon and orangutan infant, for example, start clinging to their mothers' fur nearly straight away after birth. The gibbon infant continues to do so for a year and the orangutan infant for four years.[13] Although the chimpanzee infant initially gets support from its mother, within the first few days it is able to grasp its mother's fur completely by itself. The chimpanzee infant starts off by clinging to its mother in a ventral–ventral position but after five to six months begins to cling dorsally to its mother.[14]

This ability of the infant arboreal ape to cling to the mother is essential. This is because the mother uses her hands for grasping branches as she moves through the trees. She therefore is unable effectively to carry the infant using her arms. To survive, the infant ape must be able to hold fast to its mother's fur. For this infantile clinging to be successful, it is plain it must be done with both the hands and feet. Not only does holding on with all fours give a stronger and more secure grip, but it also keeps the infant out of the way of the mother's locomotion. Hanging on with only the hands would make the infant dangle and swing, continually getting in the way of the mother's movements. It seems likely that the infant's clinging onto the mother, which we observe in other present-day primates, was also the case with the arboreal and pre-bipedal ancestors of human beings.

EVIDENCE FROM THE NEWBORN

Various abilities of the human newborn support this view. First, there is the grasping reflex in the infant's hands. If a finger is placed into the palm of a newborn infant, the infant will respond immediately by tightly grabbing the finger. The strength of the infant's grip is such that, if it is lying on its back and holding a finger in each hand, the owner of the fingers can easily pull the infant up to a sitting position. This is an amazing feat for a supposedly helpless neonate.

But why does the neonate have this powerful reflex? The likely answer is that it is a vestige of the reflex that, in pre-bipedal times, enabled the infant to cling to its mother's fur. This is also probably the origin of the newborn's ability to reach for objects. A newborn's arm movements often appear random and purposeless. But careful observation shows that, when in a quiet, alert state of awareness, some newborns are quite capable of reaching for an object.[15] This early reaching ability would have enabled the newborn to reach for different parts of the mother's fur in order to balance itself while the mother moved about.

Similar things can be said about the feet. The infant also displays what seems to be a grasping reflex with the toes: When the soles of the infant's feet are touched, the toes respond by curling in a grasping motion. One reasonable explanation for this reflex, known as the plantar grasp reflex, is that it too is the vestige of a pre-bipedal reflex to grasp the mother's fur, this time with the feet.

Further evidence comes from the human neonate's remarkable ability to move itself on the mother's body. It has been shown that an infant of but 10 minutes old, when placed face down between the mother's breasts, can, all on its own, make its way over to one of the nipples. This is done in order to start breast-feeding and gazing at the mother's face. The infant achieves this feat by using small stepping motions with its legs in order to move forward and small push-up motions with its arms to move sideways, interspersed with several rest periods. It usually takes 30–40 minutes for the neonate to complete this journey.[16]

But human neonates are seldom if ever left unassisted on the mother's stomach for 30 to 40 minutes, left to find the nipple all on their own. The usual case, it would seem, is for the mother to take the infant up and hold it to her breasts herself. Why then does the neonate have this ability? The answer, I would suggest, is that this minimal locomotive ability of the neonate is a remnant of our pre-bipedal times when the infant clung to and moved about on the mother by holding onto her fur.

This straight away makes clear the extent of the cost of bipedalism. Without prehensile feet, the primeval infant ape was unable to grasp its mother's fur; and for arboreal apes this would have had devastating consequences. Either the infant would have tended to be abandoned or the mother would have had to limit severely her movements, thus restricting the search for food. Neither of these options would be particularly beneficial in the struggle for life, and such a species would have quickly vanished.

Fortunately, however, the non-arboreal mother, being bipedal, had two free arms that could be used for bearing the infant. In this situation, the infant's loss of the ability to cling effectively to its mother's fur was compensated for by the mother's ability to cling to the infant.

Having the ability to bear the infant, however, is only half of what is required to make this new state of affairs a viable one. The other half of what is needed is a strong desire to bear the infant. The reason I say "strong" desire is because bearing an infant is hard work. Of course, it would have also been work for the pre-bipedal female ancestor to move about with an infant clinging to her. But as anyone who has used a backpack knows, it is far easier to bear a weight that is fastened to one's body while having one's hands free, than to bear it in one's arms. This is no doubt why the ubiquitous infant-carrying slings of various cultures were in due course invented. They recreate the easier pre-bipedal state of having the infant attached to the mother's body without the mother having to use her arms.

Moreover, not only is it tiring continually to have to clutch an infant in one's arms, but it also stops one from doing other things. Walking long distances, bathing, gathering food, tree climbing, defending oneself, hiding or fleeing from a predator, and so forth, all become greatly hindered for the female with infant in arms. Yet, on this maternal desire hung the existence of our first bipedal ancestors, and thus of ourselves. For without the mother having a strong desire to bear her infant, infants would have been routinely left behind or put down and exposed to danger while the mother did other things. Again, a species with caregivers like this would not have lasted long on the unforgiving African grasslands.

There is no doubt that the arboreal ancestor of the first bipedal hominins also had an urge to have her infant with her, and thus perhaps to hold it in her arms on various occasions. This can be easily observed in the extant anthropoid apes. But carrying an infant occasionally is not nearly as taxing as carrying an infant continually. It is easy to understand that a creature who has an urge to do only the former, might just as easily give up when pressed to do the latter.

However, selection pressures to have the mother desire to use her newly freed arms to bear the infant would have been ruthless. Therefore anything that aided in the development of this desire would have been selected for. But what sort of factors could have encouraged the strengthening of this desire?

THE DESIRE TO HOLD THE INFANT

The best way to approach this question, I feel, is to start by looking at the factors involved in the human mother's desire to hold her infant. And here one of the most salient features is the warmth and intimacy of the skin-to-skin contact with the infant. A near universal instant of this skin-to-skin contact takes place in breast-feeding. The sensation of mouth-to-breast contact, sucking by the infant, release of milk into the infant's mouth, along with the infant's touching of the breasts is often reported by breast-feeding mothers as being pleasurable, and even erotic. Some women report having orgasms during breast-feeding. In one study of 576 breast-feeding mothers, 40.5% of the subjects reported being sexually aroused at least some of the time during breast-feeding, while 16.7% reported being frequently sexually aroused during breast-feeding.[17]

Further, if breast-feeding is done in full naked skin-to-skin contact between mother and infant, not only is the breast-feeding more successful, with less infant moving and crying, but mothers report higher amounts of affectionate love for the infant.[18] This has led many health professionals to advocate naked body contact between mother and infant during breast-feeding.[19]

A mother, however, does not have to breast-feed an infant in order to experience skin-to-skin contact with the infant. She can also simply hold the naked infant to her naked breasts. And if a mother experiences higher amounts of affection in the skin-to-skin breast-feeding interaction, then it is altogether likely that she will experience similar amounts of affection in merely holding her naked infant to her naked breast.

Now, if this is true of human mothers, then there is reason to believe that it was true of early ancestral mothers. Of course, with these early ancestors the contrast would not have been, as it is now, between skin-to-skin contact and clothed contact; for, as I shall argue shortly, there were no clothes then. Rather the contrast would have been between skin-to-skin (hairless) contact and hair-to-hair contact.

In addition, this contrast would not have been, as it is now, between two variations, either of which the individual could choose to employ. Rather, it would have been based on a phenotypic variation that occurred across individuals. Thus, some mothers and their infants would have tended to have less body hair than others. These mothers would have experienced more skin-to-skin contact with their infants than would have mothers with more body hair. Consequently, the mother with less body hair would have tended to experience more affection for her infant and thus more interest in holding her infant.

It is also likely that it was the disappearance of hair on the female breasts that allowed for evolution of the beginnings of the erotic sensations involved in breast-feeding and in other forms of breast stimulation. With non-human primates stimulation of the female nipples or breasts does not seem to be a common sexual activity. At least I am not aware of any studies that indicate the sexual sensitivity of the non-human primate breasts. De Waal, for example, who spent hundreds of hours observing bonobos, lists their various sexual activities.[20] These include copulation, sporadic oral sex, genital rubbing, and intense tongue kissing, but not nipple or breast stimulation. This would suggest that such stimulation is not experienced by the bonobo female as especially arousing. And this cannot be blamed on the male's lack of interest in the female's nipples, for even in female–female sexual activity, the nipples seem to be ignored. When female bonobos interact sexually it usually involves rubbing their genitals together.

But if the non-human primate breasts are not erotically sensitive in sexual activity, then one can surmise that they are not erotically sensitive in breast-feeding. Consequently, the eroticism that many human females experience during breast-feeding would not seem to be the case with the anthropoid apes and, therefore, probably not the case with our pre-bipedal arboreal ancestors. If this is true, then it looks like the erotic breast-sensitivity of female human ancestors appeared after the emergence of bipedalism.

But why would such erotic sensitivity have to wait for bipedalism to make its appearance? The likely answer is because with bipedalism came selection pressure for the mother to desire to bear the infant, and with selection pressure for the mother to desire to bear the infant came selection pressure for the loss of body hair, including the hair on the breasts. With the loss of body hair, or probably during the loss of body hair, the way was opened for emergence of the erotic sensitivity of the female breasts. Since this development would have also worked to strengthen the maternal desire to carry the infant, it would have lowered infant mortality. This would have also been selected for.

With these two features, namely the eroticization of female breast stimulation and the pleasure and affection involved in skin-to-skin contact, we then have the mechanisms that would give rise to the early bipedal mother's strengthened desire to carry her infant. These mechanisms will best function, it is clear, in individuals with minimal body hair. In this way it becomes evident that individuals with less hair would be selected for over those with more hair.

The selection here, it should be noted, is neither natural nor environmental selection, sexual selection, nor what has been called cultural selection, where cultural values or standards play a part in determining the survival of infants.[21] Rather, it is what I should like to call maternal selection. Here a mother aids in the survival of one offspring over another, not because of any culturally dictated value, but simply because the one offspring is more pleasant or easier to care for than the other. Maternal selection can also occur with other traits. Another example would be the infant's tendency to mould warmly to the mother's body. Infants that did not do this, that contorted away from or struggled against the mother, would have made the mothering experience unpleasant and worked against the mother's affectionate attachment to the infant. It seems likely that in newly bipedal times there would have been a preference and thus maternal selection for infants that warmly molded into the mother rather than those who did not.

This selection process would start with an instance of simple phenotypic variation in which a female with slightly less body hair passes on this trait to her infant. We would then have a mother with less body hair breast-feeding and holding an infant with less body hair. In this situation there would be more skin-to-skin contact between mother and infant than in the case of a mother and infant with more hair. Because of the pleasurable experience of naked breast-feeding and skin-to-skin contact with the infant generally, such a mother would tend to show more interest in using her newly-freed arms to bear her infant than would a more hairy mother with a more hairy infant.

Further, being non-arboreal and bipedal would mean that there was no pressing evolutionary reason for these early ancestors to maintain their body hair. For with no more branches about (branches being one reason, as I shall argue shortly, for primate fur), and with infants who could no longer effectively grasp the fur, body hair became superfluous. It did of course give protection against ultraviolet radiation, but this function could be dealt with, as it was, by selecting for dark pigmented skin.

FROM NAKED BREAST-FEEDING TO NAKED SEX

Maternal selection, however, would not be the only mechanism functioning to select for hairlessness. As I have argued elsewhere, the adult sexual and love relationship finds its prototype in the mother–infant relationship.[22] In other words, the basis for an individual's later love relationships is learned in the early mother–infant interactions. This also seems true of non-human primates. It is known, for example, that rhesus monkeys that have been deprived of maternal contact as infants have immense difficulties in later engaging in mating behaviour.[23] This indicates that it is the normal mother–infant relation that, at least in part, enables the infant primate later to participate in normal mating. Why is this? The answer, it seems, is because the infant learns behaviours involving close contact from its mother which it later applies in close contact with a mating partner.

If this situation is transposed to that of the newly bipedal human ancestors, then, in the theory that I am putting forward, among the behaviours learned in the mother–infant interaction would be skin-to-skin contact, cuddling, and caressing. It seems likely therefore that, in becoming sexually mature, the individual would similarly apply these learned behaviours of naked cuddling and caressing with a mating partner. As stated by Ashley Montagu in his classic study of touching,

> The mother's holding and cuddling of the child plays a very effective and important role in its subsequent sexual development. A mother who loves must enfold the child she loves. She must draw the child to her in a close embrace and, male or female, this is what the adult will want later and be able to demonstrate to anyone he loves.[24]

But this sort of intimate cuddling can only be effectively done with those partners who have more-or-less naked skin. This seems especially so when it comes to sexual intercourse because of, as Montagu describes it, "the massive involvement of the skin in sexual congress." As he points out, "in no other relationship is the skin so totally involved as in sexual intercourse."[25]

Because of this fundamental role of naked skin in human sexuality, it is evident that, somewhere in the course of human evolution, individuals with less body hair would begin to be seen as more sexually attractive than individuals with more body hair. They would have been perceived as potential partners who could more fully bring about the skin-to-skin contact and cuddling that was first experienced in the mother–infant relation. This would be the beginning of sexual selection for hairlessness. This sexual selection, along with maternal selection for hairless infants, would then have driven evolution in the direction of human hairlessness. In both cases the decisive factor would be the urge for intimate skin-to-skin caressing. Here is the first glimmer of the human desire for what may be called naked love, something I will come to shortly.

This account also helps to explain the difference between female and male hairlessness. For it is plain that what is primarily selected for is female and infant hairlessness, not adult male hairlessness. This is because it is the female and infant who are the primary participants in the early intimate-contact relationship. But how can we know if this was the case with the early human ancestors? One piece of evidence is the fact that the need for the breast-feeding of the infant would have probably dictated that it was primarily the mother who held and tended to the infant.

Further evidence comes from the behaviours of our closest relatives, the anthropoid primates; for with them it is the female who normally has the infant with her. Consequently, in this picture, it is not so important that ancestral adult males be as hairless as the adult females. As a result, there would have been less selection pressure for adult male hairlessness than for adult female hairlessness. However, with the infant, hairlessness would be maternally selected for regardless of its sex. And this is exactly what we see: Male and female infants are equally hairless. Distinctively male body hair, or whatever there is left of it, is only allowed to make its appearance when childhood draws to a close.

Clearly, however, for the adult male to enjoy naked love with the naked female, that is, the same sort of contact he had as an infant with his mother, he cannot have anything resembling the fur coat of a non-human primate. Like her, he must also be nearly devoid of body hair. Selection pressure, both maternal and sexual, might therefore have driven the male to lose his body hair up to a point, after which there was no reason to lose further body hair. The reason why the female loss of body hair continued beyond the point where male loss of body hair stopped—that is, the reason why female hairlessness is more extensive than male hairlessness—might well be for the reason given by Darwin, namely that at this point in human evolution it was the males who primarily exercised sexual selection.

SEXUAL SELECTION FOR NAKED SKIN

One obvious reason why it would have been the males who exercised this selection has to do with the infant's inability to cling to the mother. As I have argued, this inability of the infant led to a decreased mobility for the mother, hindering her in various ways. This led in turn to an increase in her vulnerability. In the pre-bipedal arboreal state, the mother did not have to worry so much about bearing the infant and would have had her arms free for other tasks. This would have made her more able to find food and defend herself from both predators and intra-species aggression. Females would have been fairly independent from males and it is not unlikely that this relative independence would have carried over into mate selection. In this state of affairs sexual selection would probably have been exercised more equally by both males and females. With the dawn of bipedalism, however, and the female's increased vulnerability, sexual selection would probably have been more frequently exercised by the male than the female.

That something like this was the case is also implied by the usual height and weight differences between human males and females. This form of sexual dimorphism is something that tends to occur in mammals where there is a strong competition among males for females.[26] In nearly all monogamous primates, there is little sexual dimorphism. But with *Australopithicus afarensis*, a likely human ancestor, the male could be twice the size of the female. This sexual dimorphism, though in a lesser degree, persisted in *Homo erectus* and still remains in *Homo sapiens*. It is unclear why this body-size dimorphism has become less pronounced. In their review Frayer and Wolpoff suggest it might be a blend of factors, but especially a convergence of male and female economic and social roles.[27]

This view of male sexual selection is supported by both the morphology of the male genitals and the male behaviours involved in sexual intercourse. Gallup and his co-workers have shown that the shape of the human penis, especially the glans or head of the penis with its coronal ridge, along with the repeated thrusting motions used by the male in sexual intercourse, have the effect of removing most of the sperm that might be left by another male in the female's vagina.[28]

Thus, sexual intercourse, for the male, evolved not merely as a way of inseminating the female with his own sperm, but also as a way of removing another male's sperm from the female. The removal of another male's sperm from the vagina immediately before ejaculating his own would have been a way for the male to increase the likelihood that it was his own sperm that impregnated the female.

But if the shape of the penis evolved in the way it did, it seems probable that ancestral females were frequently having intercourse with different males within a short time span (female bonobos do this). This would probably mean that before a fertile mating, a female's vagina normally would contain sperm, sperm that would eventually be displaced by the male who impregnated her. But engaging in multiple copulations like this does not enable the female to effectively select being impregnated by one male rather than another. In such a situation, however, the male is still selecting which female to mate with.

There could be other things going on in this situation that involve female choice. As with other female primates who mate with several males in a short time span, the ancestral female hominin could be encouraging a multi-male investment in her offspring by confusing paternity[29] or encouraging increased social support and protection from predators.[30] But again, because of the multiple copulations and the possibility of being impregnated by a less desirable male, none of these would be an instant of female sexual selection, or at least not a very precise selection. It does seem, therefore, that it was the ancestral males who were primarily exercising sexual selection.

THE EMERGENCE OF HAIRLESSNESS

Coming back now to the naked love theory, it can be noted that further support for this theory comes from the timeline that relates the emergence of bipedalism to the emergence of hairlessness. This is suggested in a roundabout way by studies of skin pigmentation. It has been discovered that one of the genes for skin pigmentation found in Africans with dark skin—the human MC1R gene—made its appearance as recently as 1.2 million years ago.[31] Why did this gene appear so late in hominin evolution? A possible answer is that the first hominins would have had a coat of fur and thus would have no reason to have evolved pigmented skin. The original colour of hominin skin would therefore probably have been white. This is the case for the chimpanzee whose skin is white under its fur.[32] However, with the loss of body hair our early ancestors would have been under natural selection pressure to evolve dark-pigmented skin as protection against the African sun. It thus seems that the loss of body hair and the appearance of dark pigmentation would have roughly coincided. This means that by 1.2 million years ago early human ancestors would have been well into the process of shedding their fur.

If we then consider that bipedalism first began between 5 and 4 million years ago, this fits well with the idea that the maternal bearing of the infant came after bipedalism but before the full loss of body hair. The original bearing of the infant would have been a maternal response to the infant's loss of the grasping ability. The subsequent loss of body hair would have then been maternally selected for to reinforce the maternal desire to bear the infant. And here we see that bipedalism, in addition to being the driving force behind other aspects of human evolution, was also the driving force behind human hairlessness.

But if body hair could be thus dispensed with in the case of these early bipedal ancestors, what function did the body hair serve in the first place? With many mammals, body fur is adapted to the function of keeping the animal warm. Because early human ancestors were able to lose their fur at least 1 million years before they invented clothing,[33] which appeared between 72,000 and 42,000 years ago, it appears their body hair did not have much to do with maintaining warmth.

But fur can also serve the function of protecting skin from environmental damage. That this was the function of the fur of our pre-bipedal ancestors is suggested by comparing the environments of the arboreal apes with that of the newly bipedal hominins. For one of the things that happens to a large animal that moves through the trees is branches and twigs continually scrape and whip against its body. Fur obviously protects the skin against these assaults. I have watched wild orangutans move through the jungles in Sumatra. The density of the branches through which they had to squeeze—

branches which often broke, causing them to tumble through further branches—made plain the protective function of their fur. Naked human-like skin and climbing through the trees is obviously not a happy combination. Everyday experience supports this when one observes the cuts and scratches that children with short-sleeve shirts or bare legs typically get when playing in the trees. This climbing and playing in the trees is only even possible because of clothing. Any child who, without clothes, tried to spend time moving through the branches would probably end up with extensive scratches and be exposed to possible infections.

HAIR IN OTHER PLACES

The view that body hair was lost for sexual and affectionate reasons brings body hair into line with facts about other aspects of human hair. For although human beings are for the most part hairless, they still retain significant amounts of hair in other places, for example, under the arms, around the genitals, and on the head.

But why is this? One view is that underarm and pubic hair retains moisture and thus lubricates these areas during locomotion.[34] That this cannot be the main reason, however, is indicated by the fact that up until puberty, children manage quite well without such hair. Further, millions of women across the Western world and beyond, seeking to make their bodies even more hairless, regularly remove their underarm hair without any deleterious effects. If underarm hair had evolved primarily for this reason, then it seems that the removal of such hair would have the effect of causing pain or abrasions during locomotion. But this does not appear to be the case.

As for pubic hair, the lubrication theory is dubious because the majority of pubic hair is not even between the legs, but rather around the penis in the male and on the *mons veneris* in the female.[35] The hair in these areas can thus have little to do with lubricating between the legs. This is supported by the fact that, again, many women, following contemporary fashion, regularly remove their pubic hair without thereby hindering their ability to walk.[36]

It seems more likely that underarm and pubic hair primarily for other reasons. Underarm hair most likely evolved primarily to serve the function of trapping secretions in order to convey scented signals. Wyatt suggests these signals may have at least three functions: individual recognition, priming effects of various kinds, and potential mate selection.[37] A neonate, for example, can recognize the scent of its own mother's axillae or armpits, and breast-feeds better when these scents are present.[38] Also, when continually exposed to male axillary or underarm secretions, females with unusually long or short menstrual cycles will tend to have their cycles adjusted towards the more normal 28-day cycle.[39]

Evidence for mate selection in human beings is less conclusive. Findings show, for example, that axillary scents of ovulating females affect male testosterone levels,[40] while male axillary scents raise female levels of cortisol, a hormone that is associated with general physiological arousal.[41] Although neither of these findings have any clear effect on mate selection, they may well refer to vestiges of such selection in early human ancestors.

This suggests that underarm evolved in much the same way as hairlessness. That is, it evolved because of bipedalism and primarily in the mother–infant relationship, which is why no other primates have distinct axillary hair. This is because with the advent of bipedalism the mother had to bear the infant in her arms. As I argued, this would have been a difficult task. Consequently, anything that helped the infant relax and adapt to this new situation would have had some pressure to be selected for. Axillary hair that trapped and conveyed the scent of the mother to the infant would have been one such thing. This is because when an infant is held in its mother's arms or breast-fed its nose is typically nestled close to the mother's armpit. Thus, in being borne in the mother's arms or breast-fed, the infant is continually bathed in the re-assuring and comforting sent of its mother. This, along with skin-to-skin contact, would have calmed the infant and made it much easier for the mother to carry. Here too maternal selection played its role.

But just as hairlessness, which began in the mother–infant relationship, later played a role in the male–female sexual relationship, so too did axillary hair enter and become selected for in the sexual relationship. For just as the infant found comfort and reassurance in its mother's axillary scents, so too would the later adult find similar warm feelings in the axillary scents of his or her sexual partner, though probably to a less degree than the infant did with the mother. This too suggests that axillary hair started as a female trait that was then inherited by males.

Pubic hair might also serve the function of retaining a scent that acts as a signal. This seems particularly so in the case of the vulva, which has a distinguishing scent that many males find sexually arousing. That this was probably the case with human ancestors is hinted at by the fact that male chimpanzees and gorillas normally show much interest in the smell of the vagina of a prospective mate.[42]

Nevertheless, when human beings became upright the genitals were no longer at nose level, as they are with quadrupedal primates. This would mean that genital scents would have no longer been so obvious. With the female, even the genitals themselves disappeared from view. When our pre-human ancestors went about on all fours the female genitals were clearly exposed from behind and easily served to attract the male. When, however, our ancestors became bipedal the female genitals moved downward and became tucked away and hidden between the legs.

At this transitional point in our evolution, more quadrupedally disposed females would have had at least one sexual advantage over females who tended to be bipedal. This advantage was that their genitals were clearly evident to the male. This might well have tempted males to mate with quadrupedal females over bipedal females. However, bipedalism was so crucial to our survival as a species, that adaptations must have appeared in order to sway the male's sexual attraction towards bipedal females. Female pubic hair would have been one such adaptation. For in contrasting with the naked skin that was beginning to evolve it would have served to catch male attention and remind him of the vulva hidden just below.

It would have also worked in another way to wake sexual desire. It did this by allowing opaque glimpses of the naked skin—here the vulva—just underneath the hair. In this way, female pubic hair is much like revealing see-through clothing: It draws attention to part of the body by hiding it while at the same time allowing it to be obscurely seen. Since female clothing with this feature seems to increase male sexual desire for the female, it is not unlikely that female pubic hair evolved at least partially to serve the same purpose. Pubic hair might thus be considered the first female "sexy" underwear. Indeed, the resemblance of lace, especially black lack, to pubic hair is so striking that that lacy women's underwear might well be seen as an attempt to reproduce the visual effects of "see-through" pubic hair.

With males, however, the upright posture served more to expose than hide the genitals. This, along with the facts that pubic hair neither hides nor is needed to draw attention to the male genitals, and that female pubic hair tends to have more crisp and definite borders than does men's public hair,[43] suggests that pubic hair is primarily also a female trait that was incidentally passed on to males. In this view pubic hair, which also signals sexual maturity, can be said to have evolved in direct competition to the exposed genitals of our female quadrupedal ancestors. It seems significant to note here that the common experience of the attractiveness of something that is hidden and obscure over something that is fully exposed and obvious might well have its origins in this shifting position of the female genitals.

All of this indicates that the primary function of head hair may also be sexual. It has been proposed that head hair evolved as protection from excess heat on the top of the head.[44] This might well be one reason. That this is the only reason, however, is called into question by two facts about human head-hair. The first is the prevalence of male pattern baldness (along with the fact that females do not undergo such baldness). The second is the fact of the length of human head-hair, a length that, with straight hair, can easily reach down to the knees or even further.

If head hair evolved to provide cooling, then it looks as though baldness would have never appeared. But male baldness is common and normal enough. Female baldness, however, is uncommon. This sexual dimorphism strongly suggests that, like hairlessness, underarm hair, and pubic hair, head hair evolved primarily as a female sexual feature. This sexual aspect of head hair is further supported by the existence of male facial hair, something which is absent in the female; for this too, being tied to male sexual maturity, is clearly something that has sexual connections.

Here, however, I would argue that it evolved primarily as a feature adapted to inter-male aggression, probably during competition for females. That it did not primarily evolve because it was sexually attractive to females is suggested first by what I said earlier about the vulnerable condition of ancestral females. This position would not have allowed them to exercise much sexual selection. Secondly, heavier jaws are also a male trait that may have evolved in the context of inter-male aggression. Carrier and Morgan suggests that the heavy male jaw evolved as a form of protective buttressing during fist fights.[45] Thus, early ancestral males with heavier jaws would have been seen as less vulnerable, more ready to fight, more aggressive, and thus gained a wider access to females. It seems evident that the beard, which grows on the jaw and around the mouth (thus also framing and accentuating the teeth during an aggressive expression) would have enhanced this heavy-jaw effect and thus have been selected for.

As for the length of head hair, this too it seems would have never evolved if its purpose was simply to provide cooling. It is important to remember here that early human ancestors would most likely not have cut their hair. As a result, head hair would have been exceedingly long and visually striking. Such hair is also evidently a result of bipedalism as long head hair would have prevented the locomotion our early arboreal or quadrupedal pre-human ancestors. It would have continually got caught in the branches or under the forelimbs, causing the animal to trip and yanking at the hair. Only once we stood up could head hair have evolved to grow the lengths that it now can.

There is, however, no natural adaptive value to having such long hair, hair that, like the elaborate tail-feathers of some species of the bird of paradise, even hinders their bearers. It seems therefore that long hair, like the bird of paradise's tail-feathers, evolved primarily as a sexual signal. In this view, males have retained long head-hair in much the same way that they retained nipples: Both have been selected for in the female, not in the male, and are maintained in the male through genetic correlation. These serve no essential purpose in the male.

Long head hair in the female would have been sexually selected for because of the way it sexually attracted males. Growing from the topmost part of the upright body, swinging and bouncing as the female walked and blowing in the wind like a flag at the top of a flag pole, it would have worked easily to catch attention. Also, falling down over naked skin in various degrees, it would have alternatively exposed and hidden the naked skin over which it fell. Since, as is well known, revealing women's clothing that both hides and yet reveals parts of the body works to increase sexual interest, it seems likely that long head hair covering naked skin would have operated in much the same way in ancestral times. Therefore, long head hair would have been, just like pubic hair, one more adaption to shift early bipedal males' attention from more quadrupedally disposed females to bipedal females.

THE NAKED ORIGINS OF ROMANTIC LOVE

One of the benefits of the naked love theory is that, because it explains the origins of hairlessness in terms of the desires for caressing and sex—desires which are fundamental to romantic love—it gives insight into the evolutionary origins of romantic love. This is not to say that human romantic love, or even the human mother's desire to hold her infant, is in any sense an instinct or a genetically inherited disposition or psychological mechanism. The fact that a human behaviour was originally selected for in our pre-human ancestors does not mean that it is currently maintained for the same reasons. With the emergence of human consciousness, complex experiences and behaviours like romantic (and maternal) love and sexual desire lost their biological roots and became integrated into the human condition as existential needs. In the fourth essay I suggested how our existential situation gives rise to sexual desire. I have further argued for the idea of sexual desire as an existential need in *The Nature of Sexual Desire*. I will therefore not repeat my arguments here. What I want to do instead is to suggest the ways in which human nakedness became a pre-condition for the eventual appearance of romantic love. This can be done by comparing aspects of human sexuality with non-human primate sexuality.

First, although it is true that there is a massive involvement of the skin in sexual intercourse, this evidently is only true for the human primate. This is simply because the other primates do not have the naked skin that human beings have. Consequently, sexual intercourse for them cannot involve skin-to-skin contact in the extensive way that it does for human beings. That is, it cannot involve the caressing of naked arms, shoulders, abdomen, thighs, and the pressing and rubbing together of naked bodies.

Further, when sexual intercourse in our closest primate relatives, the bonobo and chimpanzee, is compared with human sexual intercourse, not only is it limited in terms of skin-to-skin contact, but it is also limited in terms of duration of contact. Thus in the bonobo and chimpanzee, sexual intercourse lasts for about seven seconds.[46] With human beings, however, things are quite different. Although there is some variation, with different studies reporting diverse averages for different groups, all studies report an average duration of vastly more than seven seconds. To take one example, in Hunt's study the median duration for sexual intercourse was 10 minutes.[47] According-ing to this data, the duration of sexual intercourse for human beings is, on average, 85 times longer than it is for our nearest relatives.

With orangutans, sexual intercourse typically lasts from between 5 and 20 minutes and thus is closer in duration to human sexual intercourse.[48] But, in contrast to chimpanzee and bonobos, the orangutan social existence is quite distinct from that of human beings. This is because orangutans are solitary, with males spending 90% of their time alone. The only durable social unit with orangutans is that of mother and infant. This lack of social connection between male and female is reflected in mating behaviour. Although there can appear brief consortships, these are not the norm. More often males and females have fleeting sexual encounters and then part. The female is even frequently captured, overpowered, and forced into sexual intercourse by the male.[49] It is understandable that male–female attachments tend not to appear in a primate where social and sexual interactions take these forms.

De Waal argues that the sexual behaviour of bonobos can be seen as a model of the sexual behaviour of our early human ancestors.[50] If this is true, then it seems that sexual intercourse for the pre-bipedal and early bipedal hominins, who probably also lived in groups, was likewise of a similarly short duration. Why then did sexual intercourse evolve from taking a few seconds to taking several minutes? The obvious answer, I would argue, is because of the loss of body hair. For it was only with the loss of body hair that sexual intercourse could involve the amount of skin-to-skin contact that it does. This skin-to-skin contact, as opposed to fur-to-fur contact, was something that was experienced as highly pleasurable in itself. It therefore became something that was engaged in for its own sake, and thus, together with caressing and embracing, was extended in order to prolong the enjoyable experience.

It is understandable that individuals who engaged in this sort of extensive skin-to-skin caressing in extended sexual intercourse could easily develop persisting attachments to each other. And it is here that we can discern the evolutionary beginnings of human romantic love. For romantic love is, among other things, an intense attachment to another individual that incorporates sexual desire towards that individual, a desire that is based upon component desires for what I call mutual baring and caressing.[51] Chimpanzees and savannah baboons can also develop male–female attachments that are based on sexual intercourse. However, these consortships typically last only during the female's estrus. Bonobos can have longer consortships that may last several weeks.[52] Both sorts of attachments, however, are short-lived in comparison to the semi-permanent or even permanent romantic relationships that human beings are capable of.

Gibbons, it is true, tend to engage in long-term male–female attachments. But these seem to be based to a great extent on intra-sexual aggression among females and the wide dispersion of females, both of which limit the male's access to other females.[53] Thus, unlike chimpanzees, bonobos, savannah baboons, and human beings, gibbons do not live in a group. This also makes gibbon monogamy an unlikely model for ancestral human sexuality. Human beings are unique among the primates in that they both live in a group and have long-term male–female attachments.

None of this is to say, however, that the individuals involved need only have one attachment. Indeed, as I just argued, early human ancestors probably engaged in multiple instances of sexual intercourse within a short time. This means they probably would have simultaneously developed at least more than one such attachment. Some of these matings would likely have been one-off affairs and not have led to a durable attachment, but then other matings could well have led to such attachments.

This behaviour can also be seen in modern human beings who likewise tend to engage in sexual intercourse with multiple partners and in multiple and simultaneous romantic relationships, even though in some cultures, because of pressure to conform to certain values, these are often kept secret.[54] In the case of the ancestral female, these multiple attachments with their resultant confusion of paternity might, as mentioned before, help even more to ensure the infant's survival and thus be selected for. Something like this seems to be the case with bonobos.[55]

It might be thought that the jealousy that can result from such multiple romantic attachments in present-day human beings would have worked against such a situation in our early ancestors. But jealousy is highly culturally determined. Hupka argues that jealousy is most prevalent in cultures that emphasize private property, marriage as the only legitimate form of sexual access to others, and where individuals depend personally on offspring for status or economic security. In cultures that lack such features, there is little jealousy.[56] Because there is no reason to think that our early human ancestors had anything resembling a culture that emphasized the determinants of jealousy, there is no reason to think that jealousy played much of a role in working against multiple romantic attachments.

Numerous biological features were of course prerequisite for the emergence of romantic love. I hope, however, to have shown that one such basic feature was the loss of our body hair, a feature that evolved in direct relation to affectionate attachment and sexual desire. For without human nakedness and all that it entails for skin-to-skin contact, it is doubtful that romantic love as we know it would have ever appeared.

Notes

1
THE MEANING OF "GENDER"

1. Giles, 2004.
2. Kessler and McKenna, 1978, p. 7.
3. Blair, 1783, p. 144.
4. Unger, 1979.
5. Lips, 2007, p. 4.
6. Butler, 2002, p. 8.
7. Chancer and Watkins, 2006, p. 18.
8. Chancer and Watkins, 2006, p. 19.
9. Beauvoir, 1949, p. 267.
10. Lawrence, 2011, p. 652.
11. Money and Ehrhardt, 1972, p. 4.
12. Butler, 2002, p. 33.
13. Docter, 1988, p. 65.
14. American Psychological Association, 2011.
15. Blanchard, 2005.
16. Lawrence, 2014.
17. Blanchard et al., 1987.
18. Lupus, 2007.
19. Bettcher, 2012, pp. 241–242.
20. Winch, 1964.
21. Roberts, no date given.

2
THE EROTIC MEANING OF THE SEXUAL POSITIONS

1. AskMen Editors, 2013.
2. Fariello, 2013.

3. Westheimer and Lopater, 2002, p. 274.
4. Simon and Gagnon, 1973.
5. Beauvoir, 1949.
6. Giles, 2004.
7. Vātsyāyana, 2000, pp. 40–41.
8. Marks, 1987.
9. Kinsey et al., 1953.
10. Drucker, 2015.
11. Gueren, 2014.
12. Kramer, 2014.
13. Giles, 2004.
14. Kramer, 2014
15. Reich, 1941.
16. Kramer, 2014.

3
SEX HORMONES AND SEXUAL DESIRE

1. Burgess, 1981.
2. Kaplan's 1977, 1995.
3. Giles, 2004.
4. Symonds, 1987.
5. Buss, 2003; Sykes, 2003.
6. Pfaff et al., 2004.
7. Bancroft, 2002, 2005; Regan, 1999; Rako, 1999; Ganz and Greendale, 2007.
8. Dixson, 1998.
9. Davidson et al., 1982.
10. Rako, 1999.
11. Levin, 2002.
12. Keefe, 2002.
13. Pfaff et al., 2004.
14. Ganz and Greendale, 2007, p. 4.
15. Rako, 1999, pp. 54–55.
16. Bancroft, 2002, p. 17.
17. Bancroft, 1988.
18. Mann and Sohn, 2005; Mann et al., 2003.
19. Milsten and Slowinski, 1999.
20. Bagetell et al., 1994, pp. 713–714.
21. Tomlinson and Wright, 2004.
22. Festinger, 1957.
23. Bagetell et al., 1994.
24. Aucoin and Wassersug, 2006.
25. Quoted in Ayalon, 1999, p. 325.
26. Ayalon, 1999, p. 316.
27. Ringrose, 2007, p. 498.
28. Ayalon, 1999; Aucoin and Wassersug, 2006.
29. Ringrose, 2007, p. 497.
30. Cheikh Moussa, 1982.
31. Quoted in Ayalon, 1999, p. 324.
32. Bancroft, 2002.
33. Bartlik and Kaplan, 1999, p. 14.
34. Hedricks, 1994.
35. Panzer et al., 2006.

36. Bancroft, 2002.
37. Westheimer and Lopater, 2003.
38. Rempel and Baumgartner, 2003.
39. Hedricks, 1994.
40. Rowland et al., 2005.
41. Hyde et al., 1996.
42. Bancroft, 2002.
43. Cunningham et al., 2001.
44. Rowland et al., 2005.
45. Kingsberg, 2002.
46. Lieblum and Rosen, 2000.
47. de Marquiegui and Huish, 1999.
48. Sherwin et al., 1985.
49. de Marquiegui and Huish, 1999.
50. Sherwin and Gelfand, 1987.
51. Greer, 1992, p. 177.
52. Rako, 1999.
53. Wilson and Lawson, 1976.
54. Davis et al., 2005.
55. Giles, 2004.
56. Muehlenhard and Shippee, 2010.
57. Michael and Wilson, 1973; Phoenix, 1973; Dixson, 1990.
58. Loy, 1971.
59. Dixson, 1998.
60. Furuichi, 1987, 1992.
61. Small, 2003.
62. Shideler et al., 1983.
63. Povinelli, 1987.
64. Dixson, 1998.
65. Freud, 1905.
66. Masters and Johnson, 1966.
67. Giles, 2007.
68. Ando et al., 2002.
69. Davidson et al., 1982.
70. Herbenick, 2011.
71. Giles, 2004.
72. Heider, 1958.
73. Kaplan, 1995; Vātsyāyana, 2002.
74. Schmidt et al., 1998.
75. Giles, 2004.

4
SOCIAL CONSTRUCTIONISM AND SEXUAL DESIRE

1. Jackson, 1999; Richters, 2001; Vance, 1991, 2001.
2. Vance, 1991, pp. 878–879.
3. Vance, 1991, p. 878.
4. Vance, 1991, p. 879.
5. Vance, 1991, p. 879.
6. Jacobsen, 2005, p. 224.
7. Jackson, 1999, pp. 4–5.
8. Maltz and Boss, 1997

9. Foucault, 1978.
10. Tiefer, 1995, p. 19.
11. Jackson, 1999; Kimmel, 2007; Seidman, 2003.
12. Morrow, 1995, p. 21.
13. Foucault, 1978, p. 21.
14. Foucault, 1978, p. 23.
15. Foucault, 1978, p. 83.
16. Foucault, 1978, p. 85.
17. Simon and Gagnon, 1986; Gagnon and Simon, 1973.
18. Kimmel, 2007; Seidman, 2003.
19. Jackson, 1999, p. 9.
20. Richter, 2001, p. 15.
21. Simon and Gagnon, 1986, p. 98.
22. Simon and Gagnon, 1986, p. 100.
23. Simon and Gagnon, 1986, p. 104.
24. Simon and Gagnon, 1986, p. 105.
25. Giles, 1997.
26. Giles, 1997.
27. Davenport, 1987.
28. Lao-tzu, 1962; Sartre, 1956; Giles, 2001.
29. Cleary, 1999.
30. Laumann et al., 1994.
31. Giles, 2004.
32. Tripp, 1988.
33. Giles, 2004; Weinberg et al., 1995.
34. Fisher, 1986.

5
GILBERT HERDT ON SAMBIA SEXUAL CULTURE

1. Herdt, G. 1999.
2. Deacon, 1934; Baal, 1966; Davenport, 1965, 1977.
3. Laumann et al., 1994.
4. Gonsiorek and Weinrich, 1991; Kaplan, 1995; Bell, Weinberg, and Hammersmith, 1981.
5. Herdt, 1999, p. 7.
6. Giles, 2004.
7. Herdt, 1999, p. 65.
8. Herdt, 1999, p. 295.
9. Herdt, 1999, p. 156.
10. Herdt, 1999, p. 279.
11. Reich 1942; Kaplan, 1977; Burgess, 1981.
12. Freyd, 1996.
13. Fisher, 1989.
14. Herdt, 1999, pp. 108–109.
15. Kaplan, 1977.
16. Ward and Kassenbaum, 1964.
17. Giles, 2004.
18. Stoller and Herdt, 1985, p. 404.
19. Herdt, 1999, p. 292.
20. Giles, 2004.
21. McConaghy, 2005, p. 1.
22. McConaghy, 2005, p. 2.

6
NO SUCH THING AS EXCESSIVE LEVELS OF SEXUAL BEHAVIOUR

1. Beckett et al., 2009.
2. Mayo Clinic Staff, 2014.
3. Långström and Hanson, 2006b.
4. Augustine, 1997.
5. Anonymous, p. 3.
6. Långström and Hanson, 2006a, p. 49.
7. Långström and Hanson, 2006a, p. 49.
8. Millet, 2003.
9. Långström and Hanson, 2006b, p. 643.
10. Långström and Hanson, 2006b, p. 644.
11. Stelle et al., 2013.
12. Ellis, 2013.

7
AGE DYSPHORIA

1. Speaker, 1980.
2. Money, 1984.
3. Pate and Gabbard, 2003; Evcimen and Gratz, 2006; Hawkinson and Zamboni, 2014.
4. Giles, 2012.
5. Speaker, 1980; Hawkinson and Zamboni, 2014.
6. Dickey, 2007.
7. Dickey, 2007.
8. Speaker, 1980.
9. Caldwell, 2008.
10. Pillemer, 1998.
11. Peterson, 2002.
12. Bancroft, 1989.
13. Giles, 2015.
14. Speaker, 1980, p. 43.
15. Freund and Blanchard, 1993.
16. Lawrence, 2006.
17. Hawkinson and Zamboni, 2014.

8
NAKED LOVE

1. Hardy, 1960; Morgan, 1997.
2. Pagel and Bodmer, 2003.
3. Jablonski, 2010, p. 46.
4. Boesch and Boesch, 198.
5. Harris, 2006.
6. Rogers et al., 2004.
7. Sørensen, 2009.

8. Darwin, 1871.
9. Kingston et al., 1994.
10. Oakley, 1961.
11. Hewes, 1961.
12. Jolly, 1970.
13. Islam and Feeroz, 1992; Kaplan and Rogers, 1999.
14. Bard, 1995.
15. Amiel-Tison and Grenier, 1986.
16. Widström et al., 1987.
17. Avery et al., 2000.
18. Moore et al., 2007.
19. Cantrill, 2006.
20. de Waal, 1995.
21. Cavalli-Sforza and Feldman, 1981.
22. Giles, 1999, 2004.
23. Harlow and Zimmermann, 1958.
24. Montagu, 1972, p. 164.
25. Montagu, 1972, p. 161.
26. Lindenfors et al., 2007.
27. Frayer and Wolpoff, 1985.
28. Gallup et al., 2003.
29. van Schaik et al., 2000.
30. Goodall, 1986.
31. Rogers et al., 2004.
32. Post et al., 1975.
33. Kittler et al., 2003.
34. Jablonski, 2010.
35. Kasai, 1995.
36. Herbenick et al., 2010.
37. Wyatt, 2003.
38. Wyatt, 2003.
39. Cutler et al., 1986.
40. Miller and Maner, 2009.
41. Wyart et al., 2007.
42. Stoddart, 1990.
43. Kasia, 1995.
44. Jablonski, 2010.
45. Carrier, 2015.
46. de Waal, 1995.
47. Hunt, 1974.
48. Kaplan and Rogers, 1999.
49. Kaplan and Rogers, 1999.
50. de Waal, 1995.
51. Giles, 2004.
52. Lewis et al., 2010.
53. Mitani, 1984; Reichard and Sommer, 1997.
54. Giles, 2004.
55. Wrangham, 2002.
56. Hupka, 1981.

References

American Psychological Association. (2011). Answers to your questions about transgender people, gender identity, and gender expression. http://www.apa.org/topics/lgbt/transgender.aspx. Retrieved 16 September 2016.

Amiel-Tison, C. and Grenier, A. (1986). *A neurological assessment during the first year of life*. New York: Oxford University Press.

Ando, S., Deamicus, F., Rago, V. (2002). Breast cancer: from estrogen to androgen receptor. *Molecular and Cellular Endocrinology*, 193, 121–128.

Anonymous, *The mirror of coitus: A translation and edition of the fifteenth-century Speculum al foderi* (M. Solomon, Trans. and Ed.). New York: Madison, 1990.

AskMen Editors (2013). Best sex positions to improve your sex life. http://www.askmen.com/dating/love_tip_250/274_love_tip.html. Retrieved 23 October 2013.

Aucoin, M. W. and Wassersug, R. J. 2006. The sexuality and social performance of androgen-deprived (castrated) men throughout history: Implications for modern day cancer patients. *Social Science and Medicine*, 63, 3162–3173.

Augustine (1997). On the good of marriage. In E. Clark (Ed.), *St Augustine on Marriage and Sexuality* (pp. 34–42). Washington, DC: Catholic University of America Press.

Avery, M. D., Duckett L., and Frantzich C. R. (2000). The experience of sexuality during breast-feeding among primiparous women. *Journal of Midwifery & Woman's Health*, 45, 227–237.

Ayalah, D. and Wenstock, I. J. (1979). *Breasts: Women speak about their breasts and their lives*. London: Hutchinson.

Ayalon, D. (1999). *Eunuchs, caliphs and sultans: A study in power relations*. Jerusalem: Magna Press.

Baal, J. van (1966). *Dema: Description and analysis of Marind-anim culture*. The Hague: Martinus Nijhoff.

Bagetel, C. J., Heiman, J. R., River, J. E., and Bremmer, W. J. (1994). Effect of testosterone in and estradiol on sexual behavior in young men. *Journal of Clinical Endocrinology and Metabolism*, 78, 711–716.

Bancroft, J. (1988). Reproductive hormones and male sexual function. In J. M. A. Sitsen (Ed.), *Handbook of sexology: Vol. 2. The pharmacology and endocrinology of sexual function* (pp. 297–315). New York: Elsevier Science Publishers.

Bancroft, J. (2002). Biological factors in human sexuality. *The Journal of Sex Research*, 39, 15–21.

Bard, K. A. (1995). Parenting in primates. In M. H. Bornstein (Ed.), *Handbook of Parenting: Vol. 2. Biology and Ecology of Parenting* (pp. 27–58), Mahwah, NJ: Erlbaum.

Bartlik, B. and Kaplan, H.S. (1999). Introduction. In S. Rako (1999). *The hormone of desire: The truth about testosterone, sexuality, and menopause*. New York: Three Rivers Press.

Beauvoir, S. de. (1989). *The second sex* (H.M. Parshley, Trans. and Ed.). New York: Vintage.

Beckett, M. K., Elliott, M. N., Martino, S., Kanouse, D. E., Corona, R., Klein, D. J., and Schuster, M. A. (2010). Timing of parent and child communication about sexuality relative to children's sexual behaviors. *Pediatrics*, 125, 35–42.

Bell, A. P., Weinberg, M. S., and Hammersmith, S. K. (1981). *Sexual preference*. Bloomington, IN: Indiana University Press.

Bettcher, T. M. (2012). Trans women and the meaning of "woman." In N. Power, R. Halwani, and A. Soble (Eds), *Philosophy of sex: Contemporary readings* (6th edn) (pp. 233–250). New York: Rowman & Littlefield.

Blair, H. (1783). *Lectures on rhetoric and belles lettres*, Vol. 1. London: W. Strathan.

Blanchard, R, Clemmensen, L. H., and Steiner, B. S. (1987). Heterosexual and homosexual gender dysphoria. *Archives of Sexual Behavior*, 16, 139–152.

Blanchard, R. (2005). Early history of the concept of autogynephilia. *Archives of Sexual Behavior*, 34, 439–446.

Boesch C. and Boesch H. (1984). Mental maps in chimpanzees: An analysis of hammer transports for nut cracking. *Primates*, 25, 160–170.

Burgess, A. W. (1981). Physician sexual misconduct and patients' responses. *American Journal of Psychiatry*, 138, 1335–1342.

Buss, D. M. (2003). *The evolution of desire: Strategies of human mating* (Rev. edn). New York: Basic Books.

Butler, J. (2002). *Gender trouble: Feminism and the subversion of identity*. London: Taylor & Francis.

Caldwell, J. C. (2008). Relational aspects of maladaptive diaper-wearing and treatment with couples therapy. *Sexual and Relationship Therapy*, 23, 157–160.

Cantrill, R. (2006). *Influence of naked body contact between* mother *and newborn on effective breast-feeding*. Doctoral thesis, Griffith University, Australia.

Carol, M. (1987). The heterosexual coital positions in three societies. In J. Bancroft (Ed.), *Medical sexology*. Amsterdam: Excerpta Medica.

Carrier, D. R. and Morgan, M. H. (2015). Protective buttressing of the hominin face. *Biological Reviews*, 90, 330–346.

Cavalli-Sforza L. L, and Feldman M. W. (1981). *Cultural transmission and evolution: A quantitative approach*. Princeton: Princeton University Press.

Chancer, L. S. and Watkins, B. X. (2006). *Gender, race, and class: An overview*. Oxford: Blackwell.

Cheikh M. A. (1982). Ğāhiz et les eunuques ou la confusion du même et l'autre. *Arabica*, tome XXIX, pp. 184–214.

Cleary, T. (Trans.). (1999). *Sex, health, and long life: Manuals of Taoist practice*. Boston: Shambala.

Cunningham, F. G., Grant, N. F., Leveno, K. J., Gilstrap III, L. C., and Wenstrom, K. D. (2001). *Williams obstetrics* (21st edn). McGraw-Hill.

Cutler, W. B., Preti, G., Krieger, A., Huggins, G. R., Garcia, C. R. and Lawley, H. J. (1986). Human axillary secretions influence women's menstrual cycles: The role of donor extract from men. *Hormones and Behavior*, 20, 463–473.

Darwin, C. (1871). *The descent of man, and selection in relation to sex*, Vol. 2. London: John Murray.

Davenport, W. (1965). Sexual patterns and their regulation in a society of the southwest Pacific. In F. A. Beach (Ed.), *Sex and behaviour* (pp. 164–207). New York: John Wiley.

Davenport, W. (1977). Sex in cross-cultural perspective. In F. A. Beach and M. Diamond (Eds), *Human sexuality in four perspectives* (pp. 155–163). Baltimore: Johns Hopkins University Press.

Davenport, W. H. (1987). An anthropological approach. In J. H. Geer and W. T. O'Donohue (Eds), *Theories of human sexuality* (pp. 197–236). New York: Plenum Press.

Davidson, J. M. (1980). Hormones and sexual behavior in the male. In D. T. Krieger and J. C. Hughes (Eds), *Neuroendocrinology: The interrelationship of the body's two major integra-*

tive systems—in normal physiology and clinical disease (pp. 232–238). Sunderland, MA: Sinauer.

Davidson, J. M., Kwan, M., and Greenleaf, W. J. (1982). Hormone replacement and sexuality in men. *Clinics in Endocrinology and Metabolism*, 11, 600–623.

Davis, S. R., Davison, S. L., Donath, S., and Bell, R. J. (2005). Circulating androgen levels and self-reported sexual function in women. *Journal of the American Medical Association*, 294, 91–96.

de Marquiegui, A. and Huish, M. (1999). A woman's sexual life after an operation. *British Medical Journal*, 318, 178–181.

de Waal, F. (1995). Bonobo sex and society: The behavior of a close relative challenges assumptions about male supremacy in human evolution. *Scientific American* (March), 82–88.

Deacon, A. B. (1934). *Malekula: A vanishing people in the New Hebrides*. London: Routledge.

Dickey, R. (2007). Commentary on "Adult Baby Syndrome" by Evcimen and Gratz (2006). *Archives of Sexual Behavior*, 36, 131–132.

Dixson, A. F. (1990). Observations on neuroendocrine control of sexual behaviour in the male common marmoset (*Callithrix jacchus*). In J. Balthazart (Ed.), *Hormones, Brain and Behaviour* (Vol. 2, pp. 63–74). Basel, Switzerland: Karger.

Dixson, A. F. (1998). *Primate sexuality: Comparative studies of the prosimians, monkeys, apes, and human beings*. Oxford: Oxford University Press.

Docter, R. F. (1988). *Transvestites and transsexuals: Toward a theory of cross-gender behavior*. New York: Plenum.

Drucker, A. (2015). This is the sex position women love most. http://www.maxim.com/maxim-man/these-is-womens-favorite-sex-position-2015-9. Retrieved 2 September 2016.

Eduardo b. Ottoni, E. B. and Izar, P. C. (2008). Capuchin monkey tool use: Overview and implications. *Evolutionary Anthropology*, 17, 171–178.

Ellis, M. (2013). Sex addiction "not a real disorder." http://www.medicalnewstoday.com/articles/263750.php. Retrieved 16 September 2016.

Evcimen, H., and Gratz, S. (2006). Adult baby syndrome. *Archives of Sexual Behavior*, 35, 115–116.

Fariello, C. F. (Ed.) (2013). *The lovers' guide illustrated encyclopedia* (Revised edn), Boca Raton, FL: Lifetime Publishing.

Festinger, L. (1957). *A theory of cognitive dissonance*. Stanford, CA: Stanford University Press.

Fisher, S. (1989). *Sexual images of the self: The psychology of erotic sensations and illusions*. Hillsdale, NJ: Lawrence Erlbaum Associates.

Foucault, M. (1979). *The history of sexuality: An introduction*. (R. Hurley, Trans.). London: Allen Lane.

Frayer D. W. and Wolpoff, M. H. (1985). Sexual dimorphism. *Annual Review of Anthropology*, 14, 429–473.

Freud, S. (1905). *Three essays on the theory of sexuality* (6th edn). In J. Strachey (Ed.), *The standard edition of the complete psychological works of Sigmund Freud* (Vol. 7, pp. 125–243). London: Hogarth Press and the Institute of Psycho-analysis (1986).

Freund, K., and Blanchard, R. (1993). Erotic target location errors in male gender dysphorics, paedophiles, and fetishists. *British Journal of Psychiatry*, 162, 558–563.

Freyd, J. (1996). *Betrayal trauma: The logic of forgetting childhood abuse*. Cambridge, MA: Harvard University Press.

Furuichi, T. (1987). Sexual swelling, receptivity and grouping of wild pigmy chimpanzees females at Wambi, Zaire. *Primates*, 28, 309–318.

Furuichi, T. (1992). The prolonged oestrus of females and factors influencing mating in a wild group of bonobos (*pan paniscus*) in Wambi, Zaire. In N. Itoigawa, Y. Sugiyama, G. P. Sackett, and R. K. R. Thompson (Eds), *Topics in Primatology* (Vol. 2, pp. 179–190). Tokyo: University of Tokyo Press.

Gagnon, J. H., and Simon, W. (1973). *Sexual conduct*. Chicago: Aldine.

Gallup G. G., Burch R. L., Zappieri, M. L., Parvez, R. A., Stockwell, M., L., and Davis, J. A. (2003) The human penis as a semen displacement device. *Evolution and Human Behavior*, 24, 277–289.
Ganz, P.A. and Greendale, G. (2007). Female sexual desire—beyond testosterone. *Journal of the National Cancer Institute*, 99, 1–8.
Giles, J. (1997). *No self to be found: The search for personal identity*, Lanham, MD: University Press of America.
Giles, J. (2001). From inwardness to emptiness: Kierkegaard and Yogacara Buddhism. *British Journal for the History of Philosophy*, 9, 311–340.
Giles, J. (2004). *The nature of sexual desire*. Westport, CT: Praeger.
Giles, J. (2008). Fantasies. In Y. Greenberg (Ed.), *Encyclopedia of love in world religions* (pp. 191–193), Santa Barbara, CA: ABC-Clio publishers.
Giles, J. (2012). Adult baby syndrome and age identity disorder: Comment on Kise and Nguyen (2011). *Archives of Sexual Behavior*, 41, 321–322.
Giles, J. (2015). *Sexual attraction: The psychology of allure*. Santa Barbara, CA: Praeger.
Giles, J., (1999). Sartre, sexual desire, and relations with others. In J. Giles (Ed.), *French existentialism: Consciousness, ethics, and relations with others* (pp. 155–174). Amsterdam: Rodopi.
Gonsiorek, J. C. and Weinrich, J. D. (1991). The definition and scope of sexual orientation. In J. C. Gonsiorek, and J. D. Weinrich (Eds), *Homosexuality: Research implications for public health policy*. Newbury Park, California: Sage.
Goodall, J. (1986) *The chimpanzees of Gombe: Patterns of behavior*. Cambridge, MA: Harvard University Press.
Greer, G. (1992). *The change: women, aging, and menopause*. New York: Alfred A. Knopf.
Gueren, C. (2014). We asked over 800 men about their favorite sex positions. http://www.womenshealthmag.com/sex-and-love/mens-favorite-positions. Retrieved 12 December 2015.
Hardy, A. (1960). Was man more aquatic in the past? *New Scientist*, 7, 642–645.
Harlow, H. F. and Zimmermann, R. R. (1958). The development of affectional responses in infant monkeys. *Proceedings of the American Philosophical Society*, 102, 501–509.
Harris, J. R. (2006). Parental selection: A third selection process in the evolution of human hairlessness and skin color. *Medical Hypotheses*, 66, 1053–1059.
Hawkinson, K. and Zamboni, B. D. (2014). Adult baby/diaper lovers: An exploratory study of an online community sample. *Archives of Sexual Behavior*, 43, 863–877.
Hedricks, C. A. (1994). Female sexual activity across the human menstrual cycle. *Annual Review of Sex Research*, 5, 122–172.
Heider, F. (1958). *The psychology of interpersonal relations*. New York: Wiley.
Herbenick, D. (2011). Q&A: I get aroused during gynecological exams.http://kinseyconfidential.org/aroused-gyn-exams/. Retrieved 16 August 2016.
Herbenick, D., Schick, V., Reece, M., Sanders, S., and Fortenberry, J. D. (2010). Pubic hair removal among women in the United States: Prevalence, methods, and characteristics. *Journal of Sexual Medicine*, 7, 3322–3330.
Herdt, G. (1999). *Sambia sexual culture: Essays from the field*. Chicago: Chicago University Press.
Hewes, G. W. (1961). Food transport and the origin of hominin bipedalism. *American Anthropologist*, 63, 687–710.
Hunt, M. (1974). *Sexual behavior in the 1970s*. Chicago: Playboy Press.
Hupka, R. B. (1981). Cultural determinants of jealousy. *Alternative Lifestyles*, 4, 310–356.
Hyde, J. S., Delamater, J., Plant, E. A., and Byrd, J. M. (1996). Sexuality during pregnancy and the postpartum year. *The Journal of Sex Research*, 33, 143–151.
Islam, M. A. and Feeroz, M. M. (1992). Ecology of hoolock gibbon of bangladesh. *Primates*, 33, 451–464.
Jablonski, N. G. (2010). The naked truth. *Scientific American* (February), 42–49.
Jacobsen, R. (2005). Desire, Sexual. In Alan Soble (Ed.), *Sex from Plato to Paglia: A philosophical encyclopedia* (pp. 222–228). Westport, CT: Greenwood.

Jolly, C. (1970). The seed-eaters: A new model of hominin differentiation based on a baboon analogy. *Man*, 5, 5–28.
Kaplan, G. and Rogers, L. J. (1999). *The orang-utans*. London: Allen and Unwin.
Kaplan, H. S. (1977). Hypoactive sexual desire. *Journal of Sex and Marital Therapy*, 3, 3–9.
Kaplan, H. S. (1995). *The sexual desire disorders: Dysfunctional regulation of sexual motivation*. New York: Brunner/Mazel.
Kasai, K. (1995). *Nihon josei no gaiseishokuki* [*External genitalia of Japanese females*]. Tokyo: Free Press.
Keefe, D. L. (2002). Sex hormones and neural mechanisms. *Archives of Sexual Behavior*, 31, 401–403.
Kessler, S. J., and McKenna, W. (1978). *Gender: An ethnomethodological approach*. New York: Wiley.
Kimmel, M. S. (Ed.) (2007). *The sexual self: The construction of sexual scripts*. Nashville: Vanderbilt University Press.
Kingsberg, S. A. (2002). The impact of aging on sexual function of women and their partners. *Archives of Sexual Behavior*, 31, 431–437.
Kingston, J. D., Marino, B. D. and Hill, A. (1994). Isotopic evidence of neogene hominin paleoenvironments in Kenya Rift Valley. *Science*, 264, 955–959.
Kinsey, A. C., Pomeroy, W. B., Martin, C. E., and Gebhard, P. H. (1953). *Sexual behavior in the human female*. Philadelphia: W. B. Saunders.
Kittler, R., Kayser, M., and Stoneking, M. (2003). Molecular evolution of Pediculus humanus and the origin of clothing. *Current Biology*, 13, 1414–1417.
Kramer, J. (2014). Real women have spoken: This is why we love the missionary position. http://www.glamour.com/story/real-women-have-spoken-this-is. Retrieved 16 June 2015.
Lao tzu (1962). The Tao Te Ching of Lao Tze. In J. Legge (Trans. and Ed.), *The Texts of Taoism*, Vol. 1, New York: Dover.
Långström, N. and Hanson, R. K. (2006a). High rates of sexual behaviour in the general population: Correlates and predictors. *Archives of Sexual Behaviour*, 35, 37–52.
Långström, N. and Hanson, R. K. (2006b). Population correlates are relevant to understanding hypersexuality: A response to Giles. *Archives of Sexual Behaviour*, 35, 643–644.
Laumann, E., Gagnon, J., Michael, R., and Michael, S. (1994). *The social organization of sexuality: Sexual practices in the United States*. Chicago: Chicago University Press.
Lawrence, A. (2011). Do some men who desire sex reassignment have a mental disorder? Comment on Meyer-Bahlburg (2010). *Archives of Sexual Behavior*, 40, 651–654.
Lawrence, A. (2014). *Men trapped in men's bodies: Narratives of autogynephilic transsexualism*. New York: Springer-Verlag.
Levin, R. J. (2002). Human female sexual arousal, *Archives of Sexual Behavior*, 31, 405–411.
Lewis, B., Jurmain, R., and Kilgore, L. (2010). *Understanding humans: Introduction to physical anthropology and archaeology* (10th edn). Belmont, CA: Wadsworth.
Lieblum, S. R, and Rosen, R. C. (Eds) (2000). *Principles and practices of sex therapy* (3rd edn), New York: Guilford Press.
Lindenfors P., Gittleman J. L., and Jones K. E. (2007). Sexual size dimorphism in mammals. In D. J. Fairbairn, W. U., Blanckenhorn, and, T. Székely (Eds), *Sex, size, and gender roles: evolutionary studies of sexual size dimorphism* (pp. 16–26). Oxford: Oxford University Press.
Lips, H. (2007). *Sex and gender* (6th edn). Mountain View, CA: Mayfield.
Loy, S. (1971). Estrous behavior of free-ranging Rhesus Monkeys (*Macaca Mulatta*). *Primates*, 12, 1–31.
Lupa, (2007). *A field guide to otherkin*. Stafford, UK: Megalithica Books.
Maltz, W. and Boss, S. (1997). *The garden of desire: The intimate world of women's sexual fantasies*. New York: Broadway books.
Mann, K. and Sohn, M. (2005). Spontane nächtliche Erektionen—Physiologie und klinische Anwendungen. *Somnologie - Schlafforschung und Schlafmedizin*, 9, 119–126.
Mann, K., Pankok, J., Connemann, B., and Röschke, J. (2003). Temporal relationship between nocturnal erections and rapid eye movement episodes in healthy men. *Neuropsychobiology*, 47, 109–114.

Masters, W. and Johnson, V. (1966). *Human sexual response*. Boston: Little, Brown and Co.

Mayo Clinic Staff (2014). Sex education: Talking to your school-age child about sex. http://www.mayoclinic.org/healthy-lifestyle/sexual-health/in-depth/sex-education/art-20046025?pg=1. Retrieved 2 July 2015.

McConaghy, N. (2005). Time to abandon the gay/heterosexual dichotomy? *Archives of Sexual Behavior*, 34, pp.1–2.

Michael, R. P. and Wilson, M. (1973). Effects of castration and hormone replacement in fully adult rhesus monkeys (*Macaca mulatta*). *Endocrinology*, 95, 150–159.

Miller, S. L. and Maner, J. K. (2009). Scent of a woman: Men's testosterone responses to olfactory ovulation cues. *Psychological Science*, 1, 276–283.

Millet, C. (2003). *The sexual life of Catherine M* (A. Hunter, Trans.). London: Corgi.

Milsten, R. and Slowinski, J. (1999). *The sexual male: Problems and solutions*. New York: W. W. Norton.

Mitani, J. C. (1984). The behavioral regulation of monogamy in gibbons Hylobates muelleri. *Behavioral Ecology and Sociobiology*, 15, 225–230.

Money, J. (1984). Paraphilias: Phenomenology and classification. *American Journal of psychotherapy*, 38, 164–179.

Money, J. and Ehrhardt, A. A. (1972). *Man and woman, boy and girl: The differentiation and dimorphism of gender identity from conception to birth*. Baltimore: Johns Hopkins University Press.

Montagu, A. (1972). *Touching: The human significance of the skin*. New York: Harper and Row.

Moore, E. R., Anderson, G. C., and Bergman, N. (2007). Early skin-to-skin contact for mothers and their healthy newborn infants. *Cochrane Database of Systematic Reviews*, 3, CD00 3519. doi: 10.1002/14651858.CD003519.pub2.

Morgan, E. (1997). *The aquatic ape hypothesis*. London: Souvenir Press.

Morrow, R. (1995). Sexuality as discourse beyond Foucault's constructionism. *Journal of Sociology*, 31, 15–31.

Muehlenhard, C. and Shippee, S.K. (2010). Men's and women's reports of pretending orgasm, *The Journal of Sex Research*, 47, 552.

Oakley K (1961). On man's use of fire, with comments on tool-making and hunting. In Washburn, S. L. (Ed.), *Social life of early man* (pp. 176–193). Chicago: Aldine.

Pagel M. and Bodmer, W. (2003). A naked ape would have fewer parasites. *Proceedings of the Royal Society of London*, B, 270, S 117–119.

Panzer, C., Wise, S., Fantini, G., Kang, D., Munarriz, R., Guay, A., and Goldstein, I. (2006). Impact of oral contraceptives on sex hormone-binding globulin and androgen levels: A retrospective study in women with sexual dysfunction. *The Journal of Sexual Medicine*, 3, 104–113.

Parker, R. and Easton, D. (1998). Sexuality, culture, and political economy: Recent developments in anthropological and cross-cultural sex research, *Annual Review of Sex Research*, 9, 1–9.

Pate, J. and Gabbard, G. (2003). Adult baby syndrome. *American Journal of Psychiatry*, 160, 1932–1936.

Pfaff, D., Phillips, I. A., and Rubin, R. T. (2004). *Principles of hormone/behavior relations*. Amsterdam: Elsevier Academic Press.

Phoenix, C. H. (1973). The role of testosterone in the sexual behavior of laboratory male rhesus. In C. H. Phoenix (Ed.), *Symposium: IVth International congress of primatology* (pp. 99–122). Basel, Switzerland: Karger.

Pillemer, D. B. (1998). What is remembered about early childhood events? *Clinical Psychology Review*, 18, 895–913.

Post, P. W., Szabó, G. and Keeling, M. E (1975). A quantitative and morphological study of the pigmentary system of the chimpanzee with the light and electron microscope. *American Journal of Physical Anthropology*, 43, 435–444.

Povinelli, D. J. (1987). Monkeys, apes, mirrors and minds: The evolution of self-awareness in primates. *Human Evolution*, 2, 493–509.

Rako, S. (1999). *The hormone of desire: The truth about testosterone, sexuality, and menopause*. New York: Three Rivers Press.

Regan, P. C. 1999. Hormonal correlates and causes of sexual desire: A review. *The Canadian. Journal of Human Sexuality*, 8, 8–16.

Reich, W. (1941). *The function of the orgasm: The discovery of the orgone*. (T. P. Wolfe, Trans.). Meridian: New York (1971).

Reichard, U. and Sommer, V. (1997). Group encounters in wild gibbons (*Hylobates lar*): Agonism, affiliation, and the concept of infanticide. *Behaviour* 134, 1135–1174.

Rempel, J. K. and Baumgartner, B. (2003). The relationship between attitudes towards menstruation and sexual attitudes, desires, and behavior in women. *Archives of Sexual Behavior*, 32, 155–163.

Richter, J. (2001). *The social construction of sexual practice: setting, sexual culture and the body in casual sex between men*. Doctoral thesis, University of Sydney.

Ringrose, K. M. (2007). Eunuchs in historical perspective. *History Compass*, 5, 495–506.

Roberts, J. (Date not given) Building Bridges. Retrieved 15 September 2016 from http://www.femininebyte.org/sapphos_party/m2cfspeaks.htm

Rogers, A.R, Iltis, D., and Wooding, S. (2004). Genetic variation at the MC1R locus and the time since loss of human body hair. *Current Anthropology*, 45, 105–108.

Rowland, M., Foxcroft, L., Hopman, W. M., and Patel, R. (2005). Breastfeeding and sexuality immediately post partum. *Canadian Family Physician*, 51, 1367–1373.

Sartre, J-P. (1956). *Being and nothingness: An essay in phenomenological ontology* (H. E. Barnes, Trans.), New York: Philosophical Library.

Schmidt, P. J., Nieman, L. K., Danaceau, M. A., Adams, L. F., and Rubinow, D. R. (1998). Differential behavioral effects of gonadal steroids in women with and those without premenstrual syndrome. *New England Journal of Medicine*, 338, 209–216.

Seidman, S. (2003). *The social construction of sexuality*. New York: W. W. Norton and Co.

Sherwin, B. B. and Gelfand, M. M. (1987). The role of androgen in the maintenance of sexual functioning in Oophorectomized women. *Psychosomatic Medicine*, 49, 397–408.

Sherwin, B. B., Gelfand, M. M., and Brender, W. (1985). Androgen enhances sexual motivation in females: A prospective, crossover study of sex steroid administration in surgical menopause. *Psychosomatic Medicine*, 47, 339–351.

Shideler, S. E., Lindberg, D. G., and Lasley, B. L. (1983). Estrogen-behavior correlates in the reproductive physiology and behavior of the ruffed lemur (*Lemur variegates*). *Hormones and Behavior*, 17, 249–263.

Simon, W. and Gagnon, J. H. (1986). Sexual scripts: Permanence and change. *Archives of Sexual Behavior*, 15, 97–120.

Small, M. (2003). What's love got to do with it? In A. Podolefsky and P. J. Brown (Eds), *Applying anthropology: An introductory reader* (7th edn) (pp. 21–23). Boston: McGraw Hill.

Sørensen, B. (2009). Energy use by Eem Neanderthals. *Journal of Archaeological Science*, 36, 2201–2205.

Speaker, T. J. (1980). *Sexual infantilism in adults: Causes and treatment*. Master thesis, Southern Oregon State College.

Stanford, C. (1995). Chimpanzee hunting behavior and human evolution. *American Scientist*, 83, 256–261.

Stoddart, D. M. (1990). *The scented ape: The biology and culture of human odour*. Cambridge: Cambridge University Press.

Stoller, R. J. and Herdt, G. (1985). Theories of origins of homosexuality: A cross-cultural look. *Archives of General Psychiatry*, 42, 399–404.

Sykes, B. (2003). *Adam's curse*. New York: Bantam Press.

Symonds, D. (1987). An evolutionary approach: Can Darwin's view of life shed light on human sexuality. In J.H. Greer and W.T. O'Donohue (Eds), *Theories of human sexuality* (pp. 91–125). New York: Plenum Press.

Tiefer, L. (1995). *Sex is not a natural act and other essays*. Boulder, CO: Westview Press.

Tomlinson, J., and Wright, D. (2004). Impact of erectile dysfunction and its subsequent treatment with sildenafil: qualitative study. *British Journal of Medicine*, 328, 1037–1047.

Tripp, C. A. (1988). *The homosexual matrix* (2d edn). New York: Meridian.
Unger, R. K. (1979). Toward a redefinition of sex and gender. *American Psychologist*, 34, 1085–1094.
Van Schaik, C. P., Hodges, J. K., and Nunn, C. L. (2000). Paternity confusion and the ovarian cycles of female primates. In C. P. Van Schaik (Ed.), Infanticide by males and its implications (pp. 361–387). Cambridge: Cambridge University Press.
Vance, C. S. (1991). Anthropology rediscovers sexuality: A theoretical comment. *Sociological and Scientific Medicine*, 33, 875–884.
Vance, C. S. (2001). Social construction theory: Problems in the history of sexuality. In Kenneth Plummer (Ed.), *Sexualities* (Vol. 1, pp. 356–371). *Making a sociology of sexualities*. London: Routledge.
Vātsyāyana (2000). *Kamasutra* (W. Doniger and S. Kakar, Trans.). Oxford: Oxford University Press.
Vaughn R., Steele, V. R., Staley, C., Fong, T., and Prause, N. (2014). Sexual desire, not hypersexuality, is related to neurophysiological responses elicited by sexual images, *Socioaffective Neuroscience & Psychology*, 3. 20770 - http://dx.doi.org/10.3402/snp.v3i0.20770.
Ward, D. A. and Kassenbaum, G. G. (1964). Homosexuality: A mode of adaption in a prison for women. *Social Problems*, 12, 159–177.
Weinberg, M. S., Williams, C. J., and Pryor, D. W. (1995). *Dual attraction: Understanding bisexuality* (Reprint edn). Oxford: Oxford University Press.
Westheimer, R. and S. Lopater (2003). *Human sexuality: A psychosocial perspective*. Philadelphia: Lipincott Williams and Wilkins.
Widström, A. M., Ransjo-Arvidson, A. B., Christensson, K., Matthiesen, A. S., Winberg, J., and Uvnas-Moberg, K. (1987). Gastric suction in healthy newborn infants: Effects on circulation and developing feeding behaviour. *Acta Paediatrica Scandinavica*, 76, 566–572.
Wilson, G. T. and Lawson, D. M. (1976). Expectancies, alcohol, and sexual arousal in male social drinkers, *Journal of Abnormal Psychology*, 85, 587–594.
Winch, P. (1964) Understanding a Primitive Society. In B. R. Wilson (Ed.), *Rationality*. Oxford: Blackwell.
Wrangham, R. (2002). The cost of sexual attraction: Is there a trade off in female *Pan* between sex appeal and received coercion? In C. Boesch, G. Hohmann, and L. F. Marchant (Eds), *Behavioural diversity in Chimpanzees and Bonobos* (pp. 204–215). Cambridge: Cambridge University Press.
Wyart, C., Webster, W. W., Chen, J. H., Wilson, S. R., McClary, A., Khan, R. M., and Sobel, N. (2007). Smelling a single component of male sweat alters levels of cortisol in women. *Journal of Neuroscience*, 27, 1261–1265.
Wyatt, D. (2003). *Pheromones and animal behaviour: Communication by smell and taste*. Cambridge: Cambridge University Press.

Index

www.ingramcontent.com/pod-product-compliance
Lightning Source LLC
Chambersburg PA
CBHW020619120726
47905CB00003B/865
9780761868897